D0891937

A TREE FOR POVERTY

Somali Poetry and Prose

COLLECTED BY MARGARET LAURENCE

McMaster University Library Press

Irish University Press

First edition Nairobi 1954

This IUP reprint is a photolithographic facsimile
of the first edition and is unabridged even to the
extent of retaining the original printer's imprint.

© McMaster University Library
Press, Canada, 1970

ISBN 0 7165 1415 X

Irish University Press Shannon Ireland
DUBLIN   CORK   BELFAST   LONDON   NEW YORK
T M MacGlinchey Publisher

PRINTED IN THE REPUBLIC OF IRELAND AT SHANNON
BY ROBERT HOGG PRINTER TO IRISH UNIVERSITY PRESS

PREFACE TO THIS EDITION

I have explained in *The Prophet's Camel Bell* how these translations came to be undertaken in 1952. I suppose if I had known then the difficulties of translating literature, I would not have tried, but when a person is young and naive, one will try anything, and probably that isn't such a bad thing. These translations are amateurish, and since that time a number of other translations of Somali literature have been published, of a much more scholarly and accurate nature than these. (Many of the later translations, incidentally, have been done by Dr. B. W. Andrzejewski of the School of Oriental and African Studies in London, who as a young linguist beginning his studies in Somali was one of my collaborators all those years ago and who is now a foremost authority on Somali language and literature). However, I think it was a good thing that the translations in *A Tree for Poverty* were done, partly because they constituted the first collection to be translated into English and partly because I think they do convey some sense of the life and concepts of the Somali nomadic people. And although I am neither a literary critic nor an anthropologist, I would still stand behind most of what I said in the Introduction. My main reservation now about those remarks would be that I was in places unwittingly condescending, in the manner of white liberals, out of pure ignorance, for Somaliland was my first contact with a culture other than my own, and I had much to learn about the validity of human differences—I still have, but at least I know it now.

The book, first published in 1954 by the government of what was then the Somaliland Protectorate, in pre-independence days, has been out of print for years now. The last copies, I learned several years ago, were bought by the Peace Corps for distribution among young volunteers going to the Somali Republic. Diligent efforts to trace the copyright of the book have failed, and I assume that no one now holds it except myself, for the Protectorate government which originally published the book is not now in existence, and if any correspondence pertaining to the matter still survives, it must lie in some apparently untraceable file of the now-defunct Colonial Office.

I never imagined that this book would be reprinted, but when

Professor William Ready of McMaster University suggested that it might be of some interest to students, I was pleased to think that it might once again be in print. Whatever its shortcomings, it was my first published book.

Peterborough, Ontario   Margaret Laurence

CONTENTS

ACKNOWLEDGEMENTS

These translations could not have been done without the generous help of Musa Haji Ismail Galaal and B. W. Andrzejewski, who gave me literal translations of the poems and the directly translated stories. I should like to thank Musa Galaal, also, for the information he gave me regarding Somali literature in general, and for the stories "Deg-Der" and "The Ghee and Milk," which I have paraphrased.

My sincere thanks are due to Hersi Jama, who told me all the other paraphrased Somali stories that appear here, and who spent many hours of his own time in gathering material from other storytellers. I am indebted also to Ahmed Nasir, who told me the stories that are Arabic in origin.

I would also like to thank Anthony Mariano, for the information I received from him about Somali literature.

J.M.L.

"On the plain Ban-Aul there is a tree

For poverty to shelter under."

(from a Somali gabei.)

Somali Poetry and Prose

1. INTRODUCTION

ROLE OF LITERATURE IN THE SOMALI CULTURE

Poetry and stories are, in general, the most notable part of the Somali cultural field. There are very few arts or crafts among Somalis, but there is a great body of unwritten literature. Although they have no written language, the Somalis are a nation of poets. There is no sign of this art dying. Most Somalis take a great deal of interest in their national poetry, and almost everyone seems to appreciate it and to be able to distinguish between the good and bad in it. In their own terms, their literary tastes are highly developed. Most Somalis can recite and sing a number of poems of some kind, even if they do not themselves compose.

In the evenings, around the camp-fires, the men sing and tell stories far into the night. And in the 'magala' or town, they gather in the tea shops, and often several gabei-poets will spend hours chanting their own poetry, listened to by a large audience. There are many professional as well as amateur poets, and each has his own style, including his standard chant-tunes (which to us seem unbearably monotonous).

It is not possible to make exact generalizations about a people as complex and individualistic as the Somalis. However, I think it is reasonably true to say that as a race they possess to an exceptional degree certain qualities which make them natural poets and storytellers. They tend to be imaginative and sensitive, easily enthused and easily discouraged. They have a highly developed sense of the dramatic. Most Somalis that I have known are extremely excitable people, who express emotions readily.

But perhaps the chief reason for the predominance of literature, as against the other arts, is that this country is barren of almost all materials needed for painting, sculpture weaving or pottery-making. The only materials found in abundance are sand, thorn bushes and grass. The Somali women do weave attractive grass baskets and dishes, but this is a limited craft, since the dye-materials for these must be imported. Wooden camel-bells and spoons are made, but the types of wood found here are, generally speaking, unsuitable for fine carving. Also, being Muslims, the Somalis are, of course, not in favour of making "images". Anything that represents a figure of a man or animal comes under this heading. Since there is no danger of idol-worship nowadays, the old taboo against making images may ultimately die out, but it will die more slowly here than in other parts of the Muslim world, for in Somaliland there can be no great urge to create figures of any kind since materials are lacking. But stories and poems require no special materials other than the talent of the person concerned. Folk-literature has no religious taboos, and is easily portable, since it is carried only in the memory of the people. This last point is an important one for a nomadic race, since the Somali tribes are constantly moving their dwelling-places and must travel with as little equipment as possible, all possessions being carried on burden camels. Also, poetry costs nothing, an important factor to the nomadic Somali in his poor and insecure life.

It is almost inevitable, then, that literature should be the cultural medium of the Somali people. Although the life of the average Somali camel-herder is drab and harsh, in their poetry and stories one finds sensitivity, intelligence, earthy humour, and a delight in lovely clothes and lovely women. Perhaps to some extent the literature of the Somalis compensates them for the bleakness of their usual life.

The interminable trek with the herds to find grazing and water is lightened by the sessions of singing and story-telling around the camp-fires at night. The hardships of drought, disease and hunger can be, for the moment, forgotten. Always available, the poetry and folk-tales are as free to the impoverished nomad as they are to the Sultan. Somali literature is, in its way, "a tree for poverty to shelter under"

One of the most unfortunate aspects of Somali literature is that all poetry and folk-tales are unwritten. The life
of the average poem of good quality, therefore, is not beyond one or two generations. There are, of course, a few
famous exceptions. The poem "Bond Between Kings" is
said to have been written by Sultan Wiil Waal, who lived
in the sixteenth century. And it is likely that the poems of
Mohamed Abdullah Hassan ("The Mad Mullah"), who was
perhaps the best poet in many generations, will live longer
than the average. In both these cases, however, the poets
concerned were national heroes. Wiil Waal drove the last
Galla king from Jigjigga, and established the Somali supre-
macy there which lasted until the nineteenth century. And
although many Somalis (indeed, most of the Ishaak, who
inhabit the Somaliland Protectorate) were against
Mohamed Abdullah Hassan in his uprisings against the
British, they still have a great deal of awe for him. It is
natural that in a country such as Somaliland, the very
strong and the very brave become the heroes, even if their
careers include unbelievable slaughter and cruelty. Most
people can never defeat the killing environment of heat,
thirst, drought, barrenness of country and poverty. But
when a man rises up out of that environment, they cannot
help being impressed tremendously by him, even if he
treats them badly. So, with the above mentioned poets, a
certain glamour of heroism is attached to them, and their
poems therefore stand a chance of longer survival. But in
the majority of cases, a man's poetry either dies with him
or with his son.

In this regard, it might be mentioned that a few young
Somalis, educated at government schools here, have begun
the long work of recording the national poetry.

The purpose of this work is not to arouse interest in
the national literature among Somalis, since this already
exists, but to record poems which otherwise will be lost in
another fifty years. The work of recording the stories,
which are far more numerous than the poems, will be a
gigantic task, and it has not, as far as I know, been started

yet. It is to be hoped that more and more literate Somalis will begin recording the literature of their people.

SOMALI POETRY

TRANSLATION

Because of the difficulty of the Somali language, and especially the language of poetry, it is not yet possible for any European fully to understand Somali poetry in the original. I was given a literal translation of the poems that appear here, and without this, these translations would not have been possible. My translations are, in most cases, by no means literal, but they do remain true to the thought and imagery of the original. Although in some poems phrases have been added to make clear a concept contained in one or two Somali words, I have in no sense embroidered the original text or developed the thought of any poem.

LITERARY STANDARD OF SOMALI POETRY

The literary standard of Sómali poetry, from our own point of view, is most difficult to assess. In translation, a poem often appears to us to be over-simple, and to contain too-obvious figures of speech or an imperfectly developed thought. But it must be remembered that a great deal is lost in translation. It is easy enough to find out the main thought and images of a poem, and much more difficult to discover the nuances and connotative value of many of the words.

The original rhythm and the alliteration are also lost in translation. Much Somali poetry, therefore, may not be as simple as it appears to us. Another difficulty is, of course, that none of the most complex Somali poems have been translated, owing to the extreme difficulty of the Somali literary language. Thus the greatest poems in the language, for example some of Mohamed Abdullah Hassan's gabei,

are as yet completely unknown to us. It should not be forgotten that these poems are not a representative collection,
but only a very few of the easier ones.

Although no final judgement can be made on Somali
poetry, therefore, there is nonetheless a good deal that
comes through translation amazingly well. The 'belwo'. the
short love-poems, have a freshness and a lyricism that can
not fail to be observed. Many of the images used are original, apt and lovely. There is a wealth of imagination, and
an appealing candour and frankness. The best Somali belwo
have a simplicity that is graceful and moving, in the same
manner as our own folk-song verses. In many of the extracts from gabei, the theme of the poem is developed with
consistency and considerable dramatic effect. Although one
quality found in the Somali literary language, that of com-
pressing a great deal of information into a single word,
cannot be duplicated in translation, yet in some of the
gabei extracts it is possible to see the exactness of description that is required in all good Somali poetry.

TYPES OF SOMALI POETRY

There are about ten different types of Somali poetry,
although some of these are not commonly used.

The 'belwo', a fairly recent form, is a short lyric love-
poem, and is easily recognizable both by its length and by
the distinct tunes to which it is sung.

Some of the other forms are not so easily recognized by
a European. In the more complex types of poetry, such as
the 'giiraar' and the 'gabei', the difference is not so much
in the subject matter as in the style. The rhythm is different, and also the length of line and the break-point in the
line. These differences are often difficult for us to compre-
hend. Both giiraar and gabei are chanted rather than
recited.

The giiraar has been called "the war song". I am told,
however, that it may be on any topic, although war is the
most common one. The lines are short. Alliteration is used
extensively.

The gabei, also, can be on any topic, the most usual ones being love, war, philosophy and politics. The gabei makes use of long lines.

The 'hes' is a song that accompanies a dance. It does not seem to be a common form any more. Examples of hes may be found in *A Grammar of the Somali Language* by J. W. C. Kirk, B.A. (Cambridge University Press — 1905).

There is a good deal of women's poetry in Somali literature, that is, poetry written by women for women. It would seem that two distinct cultures exist side by side, since the poetry of women is quite a separate part of the literature. The women are never present at the gabei-singing sessions in the tea shops or around the camp-fires, and I have been told that "the women have all their own gabei". However, since Somali women are very shy with Europeans and since few of them speak any English, it has been impossible so far to obtain any examples of women's poetry. Somali men have told me that women's poetry is not supposed to be about love, and that here only prostitutes sing love-songs. I would, however, be inclined to doubt that this is entirely true.

Among the tribes, the Eidagalla are the recognized experts in the composition of poetry. One individual poet of the Eidagalla may be no better than a good poet of another tribe, but the Eidagalla appear to have more poets than any other tribe. "If you had a hundred Eidagalla men here," Hersi Jama once told me, "And asked which of them could sing his own gabei ninety-five would be able to sing. The others would be still learning."

Since the poems I have been able to obtain are mainly belwo or gabei, I can deal in detail only with these two forms, but many points of style and background concerning gabei are true also of giiraar and other forms. Belwo and gabei appear to be the most popular types at the present time.

SOMALI BELWO

The literal meaning of the word 'belwo' is "a trifle" or "a bauble". The belwo are short lyric love-poems. They have come into popularity in Somaliland in the last ten years. Their origin is uncertain. Some people say that they came, originally, from Egypt or Arabia. Others maintain that a Somali truck-driver invented the form, or that an exceptionally lovely Somali woman was the first belwo poet. In any case, the belwo is an accepted part of Somali literature now. It did not spring up entirely separate from the main body of Somali poetry, since there are older forms of short lyric poems, many of them work-songs — dhow songs, pearling songs, etc. Nowadays, the work song is usually a short chant of one line, repeated over and over. but the belwo has behind it a tradition of short, single-image poems, although its subject matter is different.

The belwo is sung to a distinct tune, rather than being chanted. The various tunes all have syncopated rhythms, and are pleasant to listen to. There are relatively few tunes, and many thousands of belwo verses. The same tune will fit nearly any belwo. Belwo verses are strung together, sometimes as many as fifteen or twenty, to make one long song, but the individual verses are not necessarily related, and they need not be composed by the same person. They are usually linked together by a repetition of the word "heleyoy", which has no meaning in itself, but serves merely as a chorus.

As might be expected, the belwo are composed by young men. The composing of belwo is considered to be the normal literary activity of the young, and the general opinion seems to be that belwo making is a relatively unskilled craft. The older men always hope that the young belwo poet will, as he grows older, desire to learn the vocabulary and style of the more complex gabei. The older men scorn the belwo, not because of its subject, love, but because of its shortness and "lack of style". They say it is frivolous and immature, and there is a good deal of argument between old and young poets concerning the relative merits of belwo and gabei. There are not. however. two opposed schools of poetry. Rather, the gabei is regarded as the natural progression of a poet, who begins with the "light" belwo before turning to more serious works.

The belwo is composed either to a woman with whom the poet is in love, and hopes to marry, or to a woman he admires from afar, but can never hope to marry, perhaps even a woman he has seen only once and never again. There is a surprising amount of this latter kind of romantic love here. A poet often writes some of his best verse to an unapproachable beauty, knowing that his love for her is hopeless, and perhaps having based that love on no more than the curve of a shoulder or the flicker of an eyelash.

The Somalis are, in general, an emotional people, and they can be very much moved by their poetry. A Somali poet told me of one occasion when, after he had sung some of his own belwo, a young man came up to him and said, apparently quite seriously, "You have opened a wound that had healed."

Many of the belwo are passionate, frank and sincere. The love described in them, of course, is mainly physical love, whereas a gabei on the theme of love will place value on a woman's wit and thrift as well as her beauty.

The love poetry is, I believe, completely genuine and deeply felt, despite the fact that the emotion of love expressed in the poetry does not often last beyond marriage.

Marriage is not undertaken lightly among Somalis. Many marriages are entirely arranged by the parents, with a view to mutual financial advantage. It is natural that the economic aspect of marriage should be the chief consideration in this country. The financial arrangements are decided upon not only by the man concerned and the father of the girl, but by tribal elders as well. The questions of the bride-price ('yarad'), the token payment ('gabati') made on engagement, the percentage of the man's estate ('mehr') to be made out to his wife upon marriage, the dowry ('dibat') consisting of household goods given to the couple by the bride's family — all these must be settled. But despite the formidable financial arrangements, many men do marry a girl whom they love, and the attitude of a young man towards his future bride appears to be one of consideration and tenderness. The woman, who is usually extremely beautiful, is gentle and rather shy. Many young men compose belwo to the girl they intend marrying.

After marriage, however, the emotion of love, like the beauty of the woman, becomes rapidly a thing of the past. The reason is partly an economic one. The man's role in the 'rer' or tribal group is that of warrior and protector. He fights any other tribes who seek to raid his herds, he protects the women, children and flocks against wild animals or enemy tribesmen, he seeks out new grazing grounds and he herds the camels across the vast plains. This leaves to the woman the work of making the grass 'akhals' or houses, weaving the heavy grass mats, making clothes, preparing the food, looking after the children and the flocks, and a thousand other duties. When on trek, the women do not eat all day until sundown, when they have put up the 'akhals' and prepared food for the men. In the morning they dismantle the 'akhals' and load the burden camels by themselves. The situation of the Somali woman is caused by tradition as well as economic necessity. Both tribal and religious traditions place women's status as infinitely inferior to that of men. A man who treated his wife with unusual thoughtfulness would be laughed at and scorned by the rest of the tribal group. The double standard is extremely strong. The Somali wife is expected to be faithful to her husband, but fidelity is not expected of him.

The life of a Somali woman after marriage is one of constant manual work and drudgery. And when, inevitably, she loses her beauty, her husband may decide to divorce her and send her back to her own tribe, where her status will not be high. The result is that most Somali women of the 'miiyii' or interior-country not only become old in appearance while they are still relatively young, but they also tend to become irritable and nagging. Somali wives often have a good deal of indirect power in the tribal group, but it is dearly bought. Since their wits are their only protection, women often become very sharp-witted and shrewd, but lose that gentleness and appealing femininity they had before marriage. The change, in a few years, from the graceful, lovely girl to the withered, shrill-voiced matron is terrible to see.

This general pattern of life may seem to us to be incompatible with the large amount of love-poetry found in Somali literature. But basic differences between cultures should not be underestimated. It is completely accepted among Somalis that love does not usually last beyond marriage, and in their terms, therefore, love is not any less genuine for having only a brief flowering.

There are certain ideals of physical beauty, recognized as standards among the Somalis. A woman, to be truly beautiful, should be fairly tall and have a plump but not fat body, with good hips and breasts, and rounded arms. Perhaps the most important single aspect of beauty in women is a good carriage. The Somalis place great value on a graceful walk and a proud bearing. The most beautiful women are considered, also, to be those having light copper-coloured skins. Another mark of beauty is the brown or pinkish line across the teeth, a not uncommon sight here. Dark shining gums are another mark of beauty among Somali women.

The Somali belwo has not such a set style as the gabei, although certain literary devices are used in most belwo. Usually, a belwo verse will be two, three or four lines in length, and with a definite rhythm.

As in the gabei, alliteration is widely used, although in a more loosely defined manner. The line does not have to begin with the alliterative letter. There is altogether more flexibility of style in the belwo, except for the fact that it is a short poem and therefore the poet must compress his thought into a very few lines.

One central image is all that the belwo form will carry. This, in the best belwo, is consistent and well-developed, and of course in the poorer ones is often confused and unfinished. In general, belwo show a great deal of imagination and perception in their descriptions and figures of speech. One does find lines, of course, which seem highly unfortunate to us, as, for example, the trend (slight, so far, I am told) to use figures of speech which deal with objects from the world of the Europeans :

"You are like a lamp and like a clock,

And I am like the European who made them."

Another form of imagery difficult for the European to appreciate is that which deals with animals such as camels. Camels are the foundation of the Somali economic system, and are therefore taken very seriously indeed. It is not considered bad taste or at all ridiculous to use a figure of speech in which the lover compares himself to a sick camel. Unfortunately, this can never be really effective for an English reader.

But despite cultural and environmental differences, the vast majority of images used in Somali belwo are at once appealing.

At their best, they are briefly and concisely put, fresh and imaginative, and with an artist's eye for picking out the beautiful things in nature — grass, trees, rain, and so on. Most Somali belwo use figures of speech which deal with the things known in the poet's everyday life, rather than with exotic foreign (i.e. European) objects. The best imagery, in my opinion, is found in such belwo as the following :

" All your young beauty is to me

Like a place where the new grass sways,

After the blessing of the rain,

When the sun unveils its light."

Such images are completely natural, and have a simplicity which is extremely effective.

Another aspect of belwo, which seems to me to be one of its chief virtues, is the succinct way in which a thought is expressed. One finds this again and again in belwo, and in the best examples a good deal of dramatic effect is achieved by the brief, almost bare lines. The last two lines of the following belwo are an almost literal translation :

"Since, when you die, delight
By earth's silence will be stilled,
Then let not now the priest
Drive you from your song."

SOMALI GABEI

The Somali gabei is considered to be the highest literary form in the culture. Gabei may be on any topic, but the rules of gabei-making are strict and difficult. A gabei poet must not only have an extensive vocabulary and an ability to express himself fluently and in terms of figures of speech. He must also possess considerable knowledge of the country, its geography and plant-life, Somali medicine, and animal husbandry. The gabei poet is not isolated from the rest of the community.

The way of life of the nomad and the specialized knowledge required to maintain existence in a relatively arid country — these things are woven into many gabei and provide the basis not only for much narrative but for poetic imagery as well. The good gabei poet must also know something about Muslim theology and religious history, since these subjects are often used in poetry. As well as literary ability, therefore, the gabei poet must be, in terms of his own culture, a learned man.

Some gabei are " propaganda " poems, and do not have a high literary value, although almost always they are witty and ironical. Many of Mohamed Abdullah Hassan's gabei were propaganda poems, aimed at increasing his forces against the British. Most of these seem to be of a highly warlike and bitter nature ("Ye have mistaken dhow-men and Christians for the Prophet "), but probably they are on a much higher poetic level, nevertheless, than most such gabei, since Mohamed Abdullah Hassan was a talented poet.

Many gabei are composed to mark a special occasion — the visit of some distinguished man, a wedding, or the departure of a friend on a journey.

Love and war are among the most favoured themes for gabei. In the love gabei, the standards of beauty described are similar to those found in the belwo. In "Qaraami" by Elmi Bonderii, the woman Baar is said to have magnificent bearing, good bones, a tall well-built figure, dark gums, beautiful eyes. But in the gabei, other characteristics are dealt with as well. Bonderii describes Baar as efficient in household tasks, virtuous, and a comfort to her parents.

With the war gabei, the poetic form reaches considerable heights of drama and emotion. An example is "Battle Pledge," in which an Ogaden chieftain swears to defeat the tribe that killed his son. The old chieftain's ferocity and warlike spirit can be felt throughout the poem, even in translation. The Somali is a warrior by tradition and inclination as well as by necessity, and in the gabei, tribal war is painted as a man's proper occupation. The war gabei are written with great spirit and with that feeling of recklessness and bravery that characterizes the Somali in tribal battles.

The language of the gabei is an interesting aspect of this type of poem, although as yet almost a closed book to Europeans. Somali is a rich language, and is especially rich in the literary field. Literary Somali is not a separate language, but is, rather, a superstructure erected on the foundation of everyday speech. A vast number of words are never used except in poetry, and these have in general a subtle and precise meaning. Often an amazing amount of information is compressed into one word. For example, in Mohamed Abdullah Hassan's "To A Friend Going On A Journey," one word is used for the type of heat that comes from a sudden scorching wind and lashes across the body like a flame.

The ordinary Somali is by no means conversant with the vocabulary of the gabei. The young men who want to learn gabei-making are taught by the elder poets. There are no formal classes, but informal discussions are held in tea shops and homes and around camp-fires. The work of the young man is criticized by his elders until he attains a suitable standard of excellence in his poetry.

Symbolism, often of a complex nature, is widely used in gabei, and the exact meaning of a particular symbol is not always easily discovered. Meanings of words and phrases and even whole lines, in literary Somali, are often hotly disputed by poets and elders.

Gabei-making is considered to be the normal literary activity of the older, mature, poetry-minded man. The young men who continue their interest in poetry grow gradually into gabei poets, guided by the older established poets. The gabei requires more depth of thought, a more complete treatment of subject, broader subject matter, more complexity of style, and much more poetic discipline than the belwo.

As well as the main stream of gabei, which follows the more balanced poets, one finds in Somaliland, as in other cultures, off-shoots and extremes, "schools" of poetry that spring up and become fashionable and then die. One poet used a lot of foreign words, English, Hindustani and Arabic. Some of these words have become distorted in his poems, and now the meanings cannot always be ascertained, even from the context. I am told that this particular poet was genuinely talented, but now his poems are becoming more and more meaningless with each year, as they are repeated and garbled by men who do not know the meaning of his foreign words. It is a pity that the gabei are not written down. They, like the other forms, suffer from the fact that there is no commonly written language here. This same poet once wrote the line " lawus iyo ben-ti," and although most people have no idea what "lawus" means, they assume that it is an obscure Somali word. I have been told, however, that "lawus" is a corruption of the English word "lies", and the line therefore reads "lies and the lie" The word was used by the poet because he needed alliteration in "l" to begin the line. Now it is mutilated beyond recognition by people who did not know the meaning of the English word. This being the case, the gabei "schools" that use foreign words extensively are almost certainly doomed to mis-interpretation after the original poet's death.

Another "school" was that begun by a famous poet who often used phrases such as "my years are twenty and twelve." Young gabei-poets, imitating him, began to write absurd lines such as "my age is forty, minus twenty years." It is interesting to discover that even in this isolated part of the world, a good poet cannot escape being imitated by young men eager to turn his poetic methods into sensationalism.

The style of the gabei is not easily summarized, since there are not enough examples at hand to furnish material for a thorough analysis. In general, gabei are narrative or philosophical poems. There is no rhyme, although in Somali the ends of words often rhyme naturally, so that one sometimes gets the impression of conscious rhyming. There is, however, a set rhythm. Alliteration is used more in the gabei than in the belwo. If the poem is alliterative in "h", for example, all lines must begin with "h", and there must be as many words as possible beginning with "h" within the line.

It is taboo in gabei to offend public taste or to use any vulgar expressions. One instance of this rule was a gabei-contest in which poets were asked to describe the vagina without once using the word itself and without offending public taste and morals. Somali standards of public taste are naturally not the same as our own, so that many things may be spoken of directly in gabei which would usually be avoided in English poetry, for example Salaan Arrabey's lines referring to a woman in childbirth.

The imagery in gabei is similar to that in the belwo, in that it uses familiar objects for comparison. For example, Elmi Bonderii, in "Qaraami," compares Baar's gums to "the blackest ink," and says that the light that shines in her eyes is like that of the moon. There are, of course, some modern exceptions, as in the case of Salaan Arrabey, who once said that if the Darod peoples tried to raid the Ishaak camels, he would compose gabei that would be like submarines shelling an enemy ship. In many new gabei, World War II is used in figures of speech — the poet may say that his tribe will fight and defeat the Ogaden in the same way that the British fought and defeated the Germans. The Somalis are very interested in international events, and although their information is often scant, they are always anxious to find out more about other countries, and are most assiduous in their gleaning of information which can be used to good effect in gabei.

Description relying on precise usage of word rather than imagery is often used in gabei. One word contains a great deal of meaning, and the choice of an exact word is important. A word may have two or more meanings, and these will all be worked skilfully into the poem. The descriptions used in gabei are usually of a high standard and are distinguished by a certain thoroughness and sense of detail.

In the Somali gabei there is a wealth of material for future research. Many hundreds of gabei, of varying literary merit, exist in this country. At their best the gabei offer not only an interesting study of a highly disciplined and developed poetry, but also a vast amount of information about the Somaliland and the way of life of its people.

SOMALI PROSE

TRANSLATION

The stories given here are of two types, those translated directly from the Somali and those paraphrased. The former were translated literally for me by Musa Haji Ismail Galaal and B. W. Andrzejewski, and I have taken these literal translations and tried to put them into English which would convey as much as possible of the dramatic effect of the original. The latter type of story was obtained in a very different way. These tales were told to me, partly in Somali but mainly in English, by Hersi Jama and Ahmed Nasir. They are, therefore, not exact translations but paraphrases of the stories I heard. I believe that a good deal of the tone and spirit of the original is contained in these paraphrased stories, as the writing of them was guided both by the general style of the translated stories and by the talented acting of the Somali storytellers. The Somalis who told these stories to me acted them out in a spirited fashion, and from facial expressions alone it was often possible to perceive in a story nuances which the storyteller's limited English could not adequately express. However, even though these stories are quite faithful as regards plot, the literary style should not be taken as pure Somali.

Since there is such a large body of Somali folk-tales, most of them still unrecorded at the present time, it is impossible to make any true assessment of Somali prose. Nevertheless, even from these few stories certain trends do seem to emerge, although these must be taken more as a matter of personal opinion than of authoritative comment.

THE ARABIC STORIES

A number of the stories found in Somaliland are Arabic in origin, and some of them must have come to this country many years ago. They have undoubtedly been changed in various details, over the course of years, in accordance with the different culture and experience of the people here. Although it is true that the Somalis are great travellers, many of them making their living for years at a time as seamen, the greater proportion of 'miiyii' or interior-country people are not acquainted with anything much outside their own country. Some of them have travelled to Aden and worked there, some have been to the Yemen, and quite a number of elders have made the Pilgrimage to Mecca. Arabia is the centre of their religion, and has also racial and cultural ties for the Somalis. The legendary founders of the Somali race — Darod and Ishaak — came from Arabia, and the majority of the Somali people still trace their ancestry back to these Arabian aristocrats. Some parts of Arabia, therefore, are known either personally or by hearsay to Somalis. These are, chiefly, the Hadhramaut, the Yemen, and such places as Jidda and Mecca. Apart from this, all but the travelled Somalis have a fairly vague conception of the outside world. It is understandable, therefore, that the character of Haroun el Raschid, who was in fact the Caliph of Baghdad, should appear in these stories as "the Sultan of Jidda" or "the Sultan of all Arabia."

The transplanting of these tales has been accompanied, also, by changes in expression. The word 'magala' is used always to describe such places as Jidda, since this is the common Somali word for 'town' or 'village'. It does not convey the meaning of the word 'city', as the average Somali has never seen a really large settlement. Also, the Indian currency previously used in Somaliland is used throughout these stories, and this detail may have a jarring effect unless one realizes that it is the Somali's way of calculating in money terms.

Characterization is of particular interest in the stories of Arabic origin, and in such tales as "Ahmed Hatab" one finds the portrayal of character realized on a very high level. The general type of person illustrated by Ahmed the Woodseller is familiar in Arabic literature. He is found in many of Burton's translations of Arabic folk-tales. Perhaps he appears in the stories of any race of people who live uncertain poverty-stricken lives, but it is interesting to note that the type is found again and again in Jewish literature, folk-tales and jokes. Ahmed Hatab is the "little man", the man who is doomed to spend his life in abject poverty and suffering, the "schliemiel" (Yiddish for 'unfortunate' or 'jinxed'), the man who is always slipping on a banana peel. He is both funny and sad. Laughing at him, we laugh at ourselves, and weeping for him, we weep for all the tragedy we know exists. That is the essence of Jewish humour, and — although more cruel — perhaps also the essence of much Arabic humour. Ahmed Hatab is peculiar to look upon, ignorant, unskilled, clumsy, and yet

with aspirations rising to the stars. Gathering his chips
of wood, he feels he has the soul of a poet. The thing that
makes him humourous to us is that we are never convinced
of this hidden greatness in him. The thing that makes
him sad is that his sufferings, unlike his dreams of glory,
are genuine. And yet he can fool us. He never doubts
himself, and when great things happen to him he is not
in the least overwhelmed. Part of his appeal to an eastern
audience must lie in this fact. If the most wretched of
men can walk calmly into a Sultan's palace and marry a
Sultan's daughter, cannot any poor nomad dream of a sudden miraculous achievement of wealth and ease ?

There are other facets of Ahmed Hatab's character.
He is a peasant, and has a peasant's guile and craftiness.
He is ignorant, but he possesses an amazing vanity. He is
completely selfish, and yet is capable of generosity and
affection. He groans under the yoke of dictatorial power,
but when his own opportunity for power comes he seizes
it greedily. He is good and bad, lovable and despicable.
In fact, he sums up a good many of the contrasts which
make the eastern mind difficult for Europeans to understand. It will be seen that just such a series of contrasts
runs throughout the Somali folk-tales given here.

It is interesting to compare, because of their utter dis-
similarity, the characters of Nebii Hhudur and Haroun
Raschid. In the Prophet Hhudur one finds the eternal
"good shepherd", the man who lives in devout poverty and
who spends his life helping others. The gentle, pious Hhudur
represents that idealization of poverty found in the folk-
tales of many countries. On the other hand, Haroun
Raschid — and here again one finds an eastern paradox
— represents the glorification of absolute power and tre-
mendous wealth. It is as though a strange dichotomy
existed. The poor man is felt to be good, and (as in other
characters in the Nebii Hhudur stories) his goodness is
apparent from the way in which he gives what he cannot
afford to give. One finds this the case in real life here, also,
where hospitality to friends and relatives — and even to
strangers in need — is something to be wondered at. On

the other hand, great power and wealth are admired and envied, even when this power, being absolute, can wipe out a whole tribe on a whim. Haroun Raschid is a likeable person, but everyone near him feels the tension that arises from having to be careful never to offend the ruler. Even Abana Wys, his clown, never goes too far.

The element of cruelty is accepted in Arabic literature, as it is in Somali. It is a part of life, and people do not pretend it does not exist. Nor are moral judgements always applied to it. Haroun Raschid gives the order that all the Birmakii will be slain, and slain they are. Life is like that. The great thing is to be clever enough to escape.

THE SOMALI STORIES

Characterization

Although characterization in Somali tales lacks the subtlety of delineation which we have come to expect in our own literature, yet it contains an amazing amount of colour and variety.

There are many stories which deal with the historical figures of the Somali race, and these are perhaps the oldest stories in the culture, although no doubt changed somewhat from generation to generation. The story of Darod, one of the legendary heroes of the Somalis, and the man who is supposed to have founded one of the two great sections of the Somali people, is a story known to most Somalis whether they are Darod or Ishaak. The character of Darod is not particularily striking. Although the story itself is of the greatest interest, he is merely a rather shadowy figure, a saintly and pious young man. The same is true of the story of Ishaak, the founder of the other section of the Somali race. With the stories of Wiil Waal, also an historical figure, characterization enters in to a larger extent.

Wiil Waal is one of the most likeable characters in all these stories, and at the same time, to us the most puzzling. As a ruler he is wise and talented, although as a man he is proud, even conceited. He is kind and affectionate, but there is a marked streak of cruelty in him. His ways of testing his people's wits are extremely unorthodox, but although he makes fun of them for their dullness, he can equally well take a joke on himself. He attempts always to make his people think for themselves. His wife is the only person consistently able to match wits with the Sultan, and in her we see all the features a Somali values in a wife. She is clever, but she is also gentle and womanly. And for all her beauty and sharpness of wits she is still obedient and faithful to her husband.

With the character of 'Igaal Bowkahh, the modern Somali is portrayed, almost caricatured. 'Igaal is a humourous character, and yet there is something in his essential toughness, his way of laughing in the face of disaster, his pride and jauntiness, even in the most discouraging of circumstances, that remind one very much of the pride, courage and humour of the ordinary bush Somali. Perhaps his most typically Somali characteristic is his staunch individualism, for although certain traits can be singled out as common to many Somalis, the most true generalization is that no absolute generalizations are possible. The Somali boy in the 'miiyii' or interior-plains is brought up with little direct discipline, in order that he may be spirited, independent, aggressive and self-reliant. If he were not these things, his camels would drink last at the wells, his enemies would be able to bully him, and he would lose his nerve when making the long trek over the dry Haud in the Jilal season with his herds. Individualism and independence are a necessary step to survival. And these characteristics the Somali retains even when he leaves the old nomadic way of life for new forms of work. 'Igaal Bowkahh, in a humourous way, illustrates this intense individualism and independence extremely well. He happens to feel like a smoke, so he sells an expensive dog for one cigar — it is fantastic, unpredictable and seemingly mad, but we discover in the end that it was not merely a whim. It was a defiant gesture flung in the face of misfortune. If the world is collapsing around you, 'Igaal says, "give it a good hard kick and make it topple over properly!" It is this toughness and defiance that save him. Despite the fact that he is a little wizened man with a crippled leg, he successfully stampedes a whole herd of donkeys and sells them in the nearest town, thus rescuing himself (admittedly, by a theft) from starvation and death.

'Igaal Bowkahh is, of course, a real person, although the story has undoubtedly been embroidered a good deal. The tale of his adventures is envied a little here as well as admired, for he is one of the Somalis who have worked abroad and who can come home and boast of their experiences.

An interesting element in the characterization found in Somali tales is the grotesque. Most folk-literatures contain their horror stories, and the Somali culture is no exception. The story of Deg-Der, the cannibal woman, with her donkey's ear and horrible countenance, and her magic whistling meat-jar, is a great favourite among Somali children. Arawailo, the great queen with her insane hatred of men, is another grotesque character. Somali storytellers seem particularly talented in portraying the weird, magical and fantastic in their stories. The characters of Arawailo and Deg-Der are portrayed with vividness and imagination. The atmosphere of mystery and horror depends to a large extent on the skill of the storyteller, but even within the actual stories themselves there is a good deal of description that adds to the desired tone. In "Deg-Der" we are told, for example, that the place inhabited by the cannibal woman was a virtual desert, that even the rainclouds avoided it and the flocks were parched and thin.

Sense of the Dramatic

It is possible that the drabness of the country and the routine of walking beside the herds across the long plains produce in the Somali a great emotional need for drama and excitement. In a life that is difficult but not highly colourful, this need can most often be fulfilled through the medium of words. One of the few things in the Somali's life that is entertaining, cheap and always available is talk, and this he does inexhaustibly and with skill. Whether in boasting or gossip, or the serious occupations

of tribal councils, religious meetings or business dealings, the same elements exist — vividness of imagination and expression, and a keen sense of the dramatic in word, timing and gesture. This same need for and appreciation of the dramatic, so apparent in everyday life, is strongly reflected in Somali literature.

The timing of a situation in a story is always well-calculated. Thus, in "Deg-Der," when the husband of the third daughter suspects that his wife may have become a cannibal like Deg-Der, suspense is built up through the deliberate delay caused by the series of questions. Each question comes closer to the truth, and the climax of the story is attended by a fine dramatic effect. In " The Great Surprise," also, suspense is built up by the delay in revealing the strange thing of which the thief speaks. In " Arawailo," no detail is missed leading up to the death of the queen — the preparation of the shelter, the giving of the spear, the old magician's advice — and the final effect is thereby heightened.

Repetition is a common literary device, and it is often used as a sort of ritual for the building up of suspense and dramatic effect. In " Arawailo ", the mother's pleas on behalf of her son always take the same form, and the audience does not know when the pattern is going to be suddenly and startlingly broken. Again, the situations in "Wiil Waal and the Wisest Man " follow the same pattern, with the wife of Wiil Waal refusing the young Ali and marking his robe in some way so that the Sultan may be able to discover his identity.

Quick, varied and often unexpected action is used to a large extent in Somali tales. The audience is always kept wondering what will happen next. In the story, " The Four Wise Counsellors ", the introduction of the hashish addicts as wise-men and their subsequent solution of the problem, are examples of unexpected action handled skilfully. Sometimes a humorous effect is achieved by allowing the audience to expect one line of action and then having something quite different happen. In " Wiil Waal and the

Wisest Man ", for example, one expects Ali to confess his
attempts to seduce the Sultan's wife, only to find that the
young man meets the Sultan's final question with an absurd
riddle.

It should be mentioned that the dramatic effect of these
stories in the original is increased immeasurably by the
storyteller. These tales were meant to be told aloud, and
a good Somali storyteller is always an accomplished actor

THE MORAL AND ETHICAL

As in the Arabic stories, we find in the native Somali
stories apparent paradoxes. Side by side, told by the same
people and appreciated by the same people, there are two
types of stories:

(a) the "moral" or "pious" tale, in which religion is
referred to naturally and with complete sincerity and faith.
For example, the story of Darod, and the story of the man
who swore falsely on God's name. Faith, like all things
which form a real part of life here, belongs in these stories,
and there is no sense of its being forced or unnatural. To
the Somalis, the miracles really happened. Darod actually
lived on the meat which was divinely placed on the dry
sheep bones each night. The man who swore falsely by
God's name was struck down by divine wrath. The stories,
as well as being dramatic, have a warning value — that
is, they are meant to teach and instruct as well as to
entertain.

(b) the " crime *does* pay " type of story — for example,
the thief stories, in which crime is lauded, and the good
simple type of person is laughed at and made to appear
stupid and gullible. This type of story is common in Somali.
However, it is always a quick-witted thievery — sheer
brutal force in crime is not glorified. Theft, to be amusing
and admirable, must be clever, the thief winning by a ruse.

There are, then. these two contrasting types of story,
often told one after another with no sense of disparity.
But the paradox is perhaps not a real one. The characteristics of guile and craftiness plus generosity and piety can

exist here within the individual person with no lack of harmony. Life is hard, and a man cannot afford to be too proud about the ways in which he makes money. But on the other hand, it is equally taken for granted that the poorest householder or stock owner will help the destitute, and if even a stranger appeals for food and shelter in time of great need, there are few who would refuse him. The two types of story, therefore, do not show a moral con- fusion. There is nothing paradoxical about them. They represent two aspects of life, that is all.

Similarly, within the same story strangely contrasting elements appear. In "Wiil Waal and the Silver Ring", for example, the Sultan makes what seems an impossible demand. His wife must bear a child during his absence from the city, although he knows she is not pregnant when he departs. If she fails, she will be put to death. She knows, however, that if she is unfaithful to him, she will in that case, also, be put to death. He is a good and wise man. And yet, this demand is a refinement of cruelty, and only the woman's sharp wits save her. To us, this cruelty, found in one who is supposed to be kind and who loves his wife, and this unreasonable attitude, found in one famed for wisdom, seem paradoxical in the extreme.

But we must not forget that in such countries as this, the power of a ruler has been enormous, and wise as he might usually be, he could still terminate a life upon a sudden whim. It was a bad thing, but it was a fact, and to the Muslim facts are to be treated as such. The most deep and far-reaching realism is combined with an accept- ance of life that is neither cynical nor despairing. The Somali sees what elements make up his life, and does not seek to deny them, harsh as they may be. If the Sultan Wiil Waal could be cruel, that did not mean he could not also be kind and wise. It is only at first that such stories appear paradoxical. One later comes to see an underlying realism — a realism that recognizes the presence of both good and evil in the world and in the individual.

In "How The Meat Was Divided", the attitude to power

is clearly and brutally shown. Here, the strong individual rules absolutely, and the best the weaker can do is to be clever enough to escape the ruler's wrath. It is a cruel situation, but what beast would not be lion if he had the chance ? Power is both deplored and admired.

Another aspect of this same series of contrasts is the one already mentioned in the Arabic tales — the attitude to poverty and wealth. The " poor but good and brave " person is admired, for example, the boy who slays the strange and terrible camel, or the poor shepherd's wise daughter who later marries Wiil Waal. On the other hand, great store is set, quite naturally, on riches and security, and the richman-leader type is admired, even if he acts in a cruel or irresponsible way (e.g. the Sultan in "The Four Wise Counsellors"). In a country suffering so deeply from poverty, this dual attitude is almost bound to arise. Sometimes the poor nomad must give worth and consolation to his own position by feeling that the "poor but brave" man is beloved of God. At others, he must inevitably envy those whose lives are made easier by wealth and whose power gives them a control over life which he himself has never had. He gives help to those less fortunate, even than himself, and then sees the wealthy merchant or Sultan able to give magnificently without loss of personal comfort and luxury. Naturally, he must feel that God looks favourably on the poor man's gift, and yet, equally naturally, wealth and security are his goals, and he must both envy and admire those who have achieved them. Again, the apparent paradox is not a real one.

It must not be forgotten that these same contrasts — aggressive avarice versus generosity, guile and cheating versus honesty and piety, cruelty versus kindness and wisdom the "poor and good" versus the "rich and clever", the beautiful versus the grotesque — exist in almost all folk-tales found in countries where life is hard and insecure but where religious faith flourishes.

The same apparent contrasts appear in the European culture of some centuries ago, for example, in the tales of

Chaucer and Boccaccio, gathered as they were from many
sources of medieval folk-tales whose roots were deep in
the lives of the people. In the "Canterbury Tales", the
Miller's lusty story could be enjoyed by the company as
much as the Knight's idealistic and romantic one. The
Prioress, prim and pious as she was, with her motto of
"Amor Vincit Omnia", could tell a tale whose religious
content only thinly veiled its cruel and bloodthirsty quality.

In the Bible, too, and particularly in the Old Testament,
exactly the same contrasts are found. Cruelty and compassion, guile and piety, the virtues of poverty and the
splendours of wealth — there is a place for all. Jacob,
beloved of God, who was to wrestle with the angel of the
Lord, this same Jacob increased his flocks and herds from
among the stock of Laban by means of magic and a ruse,
so that "the feebler were Laban's, and the stronger Jacob's."

Although our own literature and civilization are certainly not lacking in paradox, they have become so much
more subtle and complex that the raw contrasts of our
earlier history are not always immediately understandable
or acceptable to us when they appear today. But the contrasts found in these Somali stories are only strange when
we fail to realize that they are the inevitable offshoots of an
environment as harsh as this. There is no real paradox
except the basic one found in countries where poverty and
insecurity have corrupted people but have, miraculously,
been unable to stamp out their humanity — warm, hospit-
able, humorous, and of an amazing courage.

RELIGION

Many religious miracles occur in these stories, and are
believed implicitly by the Somali people. To appreciate
the dramatic and religious effect of these stories, one must
realize this fact and accept it. This is, of course, true both
of the Arabic stories (such as Nebii Hhudur, Ahmed Hatab,
etc.) and of the Somali (Darod, The False Swearing, etc.).

One should not underestimate the importance of religion in these stories. The Muslim faith is bound up inex-

tricably with the lives of the people. Religion, of course, occurs in the stories in ways other than the miracles. For example, most of the moral and ethical concepts mentioned previously have a religious base. Generosity to strangers and help to the poor — this is a basic tenet of the Muslim religion. Again, acceptance of life as it is, despite its hardships and cruelties — this is summed up in the word "Islam" — submission to God. If it is God's will that tragedies should occur, then the individual must bear these things patiently and uncomplainingly. This may seem unprogressive, socially, to us, as it does not (unlike Protestant Christianity) easily allow for vigorous social action to bring about change. But when one considers the life of the nomad, both here and in other Muslim countries, then it becomes understandable and almost inevitable.

A man may spend his life taking his herd of camels back and forth from the wells to the grazing grounds, and these may be a hundred miles apart. Living his spare, unrewarding and cruelly difficult life, even greater difficulties may befall him at any time. His stock may die of disease or thirst, his family may weaken and die from lack of food and water, or, after the rains, malaria may take a huge toll from his tribal group. Life is utterly hard and utterly insecure. In such an environment, therefore, complete faith in and submission to God is the only thing that saves his sanity.

MAGIC

Despite the Muslim religion, magic is still found to quite an extent in Somaliland, and of course it appears in some of the stories. For example, in the story of Deg-Der, there is the ear of the cannibal woman, that could hear the breathing of a herdboy under a thorn bush, though he were a night's journey away, and the magic meat-jar that whistled when anyone save Deg-Der removed the lid. Are these things actually believed here ? It is very difficult to say. Certainly, many magical things are believed in, some of them in a rather undercover and secret way. But whether or not adults would believe in Deg-Der, any more than adults in England would believe in Jack And the Beanstalk, it is quite impossible to tell. Probably a good deal of minor magic, like our own superstitions, is both believed and not believed here. We will say "I'm not in the least superstitious," and then proceed to fling spilled salt over the left shoulder. Among Somalis, magic is accepted completely within the folk-tales, although perhaps not always outside them.

HUMOUR

Humour, in all its various aspects, is one of the commonest factors in Somali prose. There are many different kinds of humour here, and some of these are not understood very well by the European mind. Some types of Somali humour, however, correspond closely with our own ideas of humour. For example :

(a) The humour of the fantastic or of overstatement. This is a common type of humour in Somali stories. In "The Strange And Terrible Camel", the camel not only eats people, but the people remain alive for years in its belly, and when the brave lad goes out to kill the beast, he takes plenty of food, since the people inside will probably be hungry after their long imprisonment. Also, the camel's cry, "The bush-country has a good aim !", when the boy shoots his arrow, is another bit of humorous absurdity. In "The Death of Arawailo", the old magician who decides he must father a son that will kill the queen, is at the time a hundred and thirty-five years old, and withered in body from the waist down. What of it ? Arawailo's daughter nevertheless bears him a son. Again, in " 'Igaal Bowkahh", the hero sells a dog for one cigar and continues his way in good spirits. In "The Four Wise Counsellors", the initially ridiculous situation is made even more so by calling in four hashish addicts to take the place of the court wise-men and elders. This kind of humour is one at which the Somalis are especially talented.

(b) The humour of cleverness and sharpness of wit, often depending on a witty and unexpected revelation. For example, the thief stories, "The Ghee and Milk", and "The

Man Who Had Four Wives". Sometimes this type of humour is used to illustrate a truth, as in "Right and Wrong", or "The Cheating Lesson".

(c) The humour of someone's stupidity. This is usually in anecdote form, depending on an absurd conclusion, such as the Midgan jokes or "The Townsman".

CONCLUSION

It cannot be stressed too strongly that the stories given here are only a few out of the hundreds that exist in this country. However, even from these few it can be seen that the Somali folk-literature is extremely rich.

Certainly, judged by our own literary standards, these tales have many flaws. For example, they may seem to be unsubtle and overly repetitive. But, like many of the folk-tales in our own literature, it is the combination of simplicity and shrewdness that renders these stories effective. Also, they must, I believe, be accepted and enjoyed for what they are — not the accumulation of the writings of centuries, but the stories of a highly imaginative race without a written language.

In a country as barren as this, where the population is almost entirely nomadic and where the actual process of survival demands so much effort and tenacity from each tribesman, it seems remarkable that there should be such a large body of unwritten literature, containing such a high degree of dramatic sense, vivid imagination and wit.

Hargeisa,
April, 1952.

II. SOMALI POETRY

BELWO

Since, when you die, delight
By earth's silence will be stilled,
Then let not now the priest
Drive you from your song.

* * *

I long for you, as one
Whose dhow in summer winds
Is blown adrift and lost,
Longs for land, and finds —
Again the compass tells —
A grey and empty sea.

* * *

A man enchanted by the waking dream
That enters like a djinn, his heart to own,
Can never sleep, Amiina — I have been
Away, these nights, walking the clouds of heaven.

* * *

(1) Woman, lovely as lightning at dawn,
Speak to me even once.

NOTES:

(1) Lightning at dawn is supposed to be an omen of rain.
The image, therefore, has both beauty and an association with good-fortune.

* * *

Do you now, Waysara, cause my head to spin,
And then refuse me solace in my wretchedness?

* * *

If I set myself to write
Of the love that holds my heart,
(1) A wondrous great Kitab
Could not contain it all.

NOTES:

(1) The Arabic word "Kitab" is used here rather than the English "book", since the Qoran and a few theological books are the only ones known to a majority of Somalis; the word has associations of strangeness, mystery and power which the word "book" does not convey.

* * *

Like a camel sick to the bone,
Weakened and withering in strength,
So I, from love of you,
Oh Dudi, grow wasted and gaunt.

* * *

(1) I ask the stealthy hyena
Who prowls past Dunbuluk's fires,
If he, from his wide wandering,
Brings back one word of you.

NOTES:

(1) There are many superstitions about hyenas among Somalis. The beasts are loathed as unclean and hated as stock-killers, but they are considered to have brains like men, and to be capable of infinite guile. The Esa people of Borama district are said to be fey and to speak the language of hyenas when they choose.

* * *

Sustenance, shelter, kindness and all your due,
You were refused, Dolweris, in those days :
He who begot you knows why now you seek
A bitter loveless sleep in strangers' arms.

* * *

The bonds of kindred blood that claimed
First loyalty from me,
Are sundered, Weeris, for your sake,
Since you now claim my heart.

* * *

Your bright mouth and its loveliness,
Your fragrance, the look of you —
Ubah, flower-named, for these
My journey is forgotten.

*   *   *

So perfect are her teeth, one might mistake
Their whiteness for the palest inner bark
Cut from a place of Allah's kindly Grace
Where new rains fell and the 'galol' tree flourished,
(1) And fashioned into a vessel, bound around
With pearls, pink-glowing, garnered from Zeilah's sea.

NOTES:

(1) The Somalis actually have vessels like the one described, made of white bark, and bound around with small
shells or seed-pearls. Such vessels are rare nowadays,
since the Zeilah pearl-fishing industry has stopped. The
image of the pearls refers to the pink or pinkish-brown
line across the teeth, fairly common here and considered
a mark of great beauty. The translation is longer than
the original, since some of the Somali words are rich
in implication. The word for 'place', for example, also
means 'Allah's Grace'.

*   *   *

Turn not away in scorn.
Some day a grave will prove
The frailty of that face,
And worms its grace enjoy.
Let me enjoy you now —
Turn not away in scorn.

*   *   *

All your young beauty is to me
Like a place where the new grass sways,
After the blessing of the rain,
When the sun unveils its light.

*   *   *

The girls who were fair as diamonds
And slender as the trees —
In the country that they left,
Why should I remain ?

*　　　*　　　*

Your body is to Age and Death betrothed,
And some day all its richness they will share :
Before your firm flesh goes to feed their lusts,
Do not deny my right to love you now.

*　　　*　　　*

(1) You hear my pleading songs to you,
But surely the drought of the last Jilal
Has addled your brain and shrivelled your heart —
Else why do you not come to me ?

NOTES :

(1) The Jilal season consists of the winter months, and is usually marked by heat and drought throughout the country.

*　　　*　　　*

She is like her mother before her,
Lithe, and straight of limb.
Her body should be clad
In fine-spun silken robes.

*　　　*　　　*

The curving of your breasts
Like apples sweet and small,
Tolmoon, I will know again
When night turns dusk to dark.

*　　　*　　　*

The merciful will not ignore
A man whose death draws near :
Before the earth receives my bones,
Show mercy unto me.

*　　　*　　　*

He who has lain between her breasts
Can call his life fulfilled.
Oh God, may I never be denied
The well of happiness.

*   *   *

BELWO — SOLDIERS' MARCHING SONGS

Whenever there's a war to fight,
Gossiping talk is a waste of time;
We soldiers must march on and on,
We are the testicles of the state.

*   *   *

I lost my ammunition on the trek,
And then I lost my rosary as well —
Oh Rubo, love of mine, come out with me
Across the plains, and we will search for them.

*   *   *

GABEI — PRAYER AGAINST EVILS

(1) Evils lurking behind us, be ye halted there,
Evils waiting before us, be ye forced to flee,
Evils hovering above us, be ye suspended still,
Evils rising beneath us, be ye blunted of spear,
Evils treading beside us, be ye thrust afar.

NOTES:

(1) The prayer against evils may contain a survival of pre-
Islamic belief, that is, addressing the evils as person-
alities. The evil "rising beneath us" is pictured as a
spear growing like a blade of grass, from the ground,
to stab the passer-by.

*   *   *

TRIBE ON WHOM MISFORTUNES COME
(Extracts from a gabei)

When fate decrees that evil days
A tribe shall meet,
Even the clouds must flee the path
The cursed ones take.
Faltering the elders grow, and weak,
And counsel fails.

(1) As a vessel is overturned to shield
　　Sweet ripe dates,
　　So from the tribe's eyes God conceals
　　Wisdom and light.

NOTES :

(1) The vessel spoken of in the poem is a two-part jar,
woven from grass and dyed with bright colours. The
deep portion is used both as a container for food and
as a lid to cover the other half of the dish, which
resembles a grass tray.

*　　　　*　　　　*

TO A FRIEND GOING ON A JOURNEY
(1) (Extract from a gabei by Mohamed Abdullah Hassan)

Now you depart, and though your way may lead
Through airless forests thick with 'hhagar' trees,
Places steeped in heat, stifling and dry,
Where breath comes hard, and no fresh breeze can reach —
Yet may God place a shield of coolest air
Between your body and the assailant sun.

And in a random scorching flame of wind
That parches the painful throat, and sears the flesh,
May God, in His compassion, let you find
The great-boughed tree that will protect and shade.

On every side of you, I now would place
Prayers from the Holy Qoran, to bless your path,
That ills may not descend, nor evils harm,
And you may travel in the peace of faith.

To all the blessings I bestow on you,
Friend, yourself now say a last Amen.

NOTES :

(1) Mohamed Abdullah Hassan, who was called "The Mad
Mullah", was the leader of the Dervishes in the revolts
against the British at the beginning of this century.
Although many of his poems are a call to arms against
the British, he also composed a number of gabei on

other topics, such as this one. He is acknowledged to
have been the best poet in Somaliland for many generations. A special poem is often composed to mark
a leave-taking, in which advice is given and farewells
are said. There is a word in Somali for "talking with
a person for the last time before a journey."

*   *   *

PRIDE
(Extract from a gabei)

Why do two mighty tribes make war,
And fight until both are weak?
Because two prides have met and clashed,
And could not be reconciled.
Why do two men grow fiery with wrath,
And fight until strength has gone?
Because one pride crossed another's path,
And neither would step aside.
Ye obstinate men, in this same way
The brother of Cain was killed.

*   *   *

TO A FAITHLESS FRIEND
(1)   (Extract from a gabei by Salaan Arrabey)

A woman in childbirth, fainting with cruel pain,
May swear this suffering never to forget,
But when her menstrual time has come again,
Birth's agony has faded from her mind.

There was a man who once knew great distress,
And lost his wealth, his power, his tribe's respect.
But now, restored to eminence, he forgets
His former anguish, and my assistance then.
Ah, friend, your memory is short as any woman's!

NOTES:

(1) Salaan Arrabey is one of the most famous of Somali
poets. He died about five years ago. His tribe was
Habr Toljalla, of the Ishaak branch of Somalis. He
worked in Aden and Kenya, and returned in his old

age to Somaliland, where he lived mainly in Burao and
Ainabo. He was a prolific poet, and Hersi Jama tells
me he could turn out gabei "like the rain". He was
a warlike man, and composed many poems against the
Darod section of the Somali people.

*　　　*　　　*

THE BOND BETWEEN KINGS

(1)　　　(Extract from a giiraar by Sultan Wiil Waal)

If thy knees are afflicted with pain, Sultan,
I also limp in mine.

(2)　　　If the cloth of mourning is on thy head,
I, too, sorrow's vestment wear.
And if thy kingdom is lost to thee,
I tremble for my own.

NOTES:

(1) Wiil Waal was the national hero who drove the last
Galla king from Jigjigga in the 16th century. He is
a legendary figure now, and many tales are told of
his wisdom and cleverness. Among Somalis, the word
"Sultan" is pronounced "Scol-dan" with the emphasis
on the last syllable.

(2) The cloth of mourning ("wiir") is a white scarf worn
around the head. I am told that nowadays only women
wear this mourning-cloth, but one can only assume
that the custom was different in Wiil Waal's time. This
poem, if it really was composed by Wiil Waal, must
be one of the oldest surviving poems in Somali.

*　　　*　　　*

BATTLE PLEDGE

(1)　　　　　(A war gabei)

If you, oh 'Aynabo, my fleet and fiery horse,
Do not grow battle-worn, and slow of foot, and weak;
And if your shining flanks and finely arching neck

(2) Do not grow gaunt and thin as the branch on the dry
    grey thorn;
    And if your frenzied hooves do not flail through the
    dead,
    The bodies piled as high as ever grew the grass;
    And if a man among us can draw the name of peace
    Forth from the deepest well where I have flung it down;
(3) And if the strong-limbed spearmen of all the Baha-
    wadleh
    Do not now fight in fury, and fight unto the death;
    And if our enemy's food is not scant meat alone,
(4) With milk gone from the land, and their camels seized
    as loot;
    And if my dead son, Ali, is not greater in their eyes
    Than his craven murderers thought when they stabbed
    away his life;
    And if the sky in future does not its colour change,
    Filled with the dust of death, reflecting the flare of
    the fray;
    And if all that I swear does not, as I swear it, come
    to pass—
    Then the warrior son of my father has become a witless
    fool.

NOTES:

(1) This gabei was composed by an Ogaden chieftain whose
    son had been killed by another tribe. The chieftain
    asked the other tribe for a compensation of 200 camels,
    instead of the usual 100, and the tribe refused. Warfare
    resulted. This is the chief's war pledge, and is address-
    ed to his horse 'Aynabo, although in actuality, of course,
    to the enemy. The Ogaden are a section of the Darod
    Somalis, and live close to Ethiopia. They are famed for
    their warlike spirit, and they still attack and raid the
    Ishaak Somalis. Their nick-name is "Libahh" (lion).

    Although it is not possible to reproduce the Somali
    rhythm, an attempt has been made to use a rhythm
    which would get across the effect of a chant. Also, I
    have tried to convey something of the effect of Somali

alliteration by making the English translation alliterative in "f". In Somali, of course, alliteration is much more extensive throughout the poem.

(2) "the branch on the dry grey thorn" . . . literally, "as the tooth-brushing twig", a type of small slender branch chewed by Somalis for cleaning the teeth. I have changed the line because the effect would have been unfortunate in English.

(3) "the Bahawadleh" : i.e. the sub-section of the Ogaden, commanded by the chieftain who composed the gabei.

(4) "milk gone from the land" . . this may sound odd in English, but in Somali it is a very serious matter, since meat and milk are the two main foods of the interior-plains people. Camel milk is rich and nutritious, and often in a good season the people live on milk alone for months. Depriving a tribe of its camels, and therefore of milk, would mean a great loss of strength.

* * *

"QARAAMI" (PASSION)

(1)   (A love-gabei by Elmi Bonderii)

Listen ye men, God's judgement, I say to you,
Is ageless, unending. And I am forever a poet.
When I am weary, and want no friend but peace,
And say to you, "This night my songs are done",
Your clamorous voices still would force from me
One ballad more to warm the dwindling fire.
But if you profit by a poet's words,
Should I withhold them ? So—I yield to you.

If you demand to have your hearts made light,
Why, then, I'll do that, too. But you must bring
Baar, my own beloved, here to me.
A slender gleaming rope of gold I'll place
Around her neck, and all my burning song
Shall be of her. She is altogether fair :
(2) Her fine-shaped bones begin her excellence;

(3) Magnificent of bearing, tall is she;
A proud grace is her body's greatest splendour;
Yet is she gentle, womanly, soft of skin.
(4) Her gums' dark gloss is like unto blackest ink;
And a careless flickering of her slanted eyes
Begets a light clear as the white spring moon.
My heart leaps when I see her walking by,
Infinite suppleness in her body's sway.
(5) I often fear that some malicious djinn
May envy her beauty, and wish to do her harm.

(6) She is like the girl that Qaabiil and Haabiil loved,
And over whom they fought, and both were slain;
Or like that Qanso of the Ogaden,
Whose suitors came from two opposing tribes,
And in their battle a thousand warriors died.
But nowadays, no man could hope to find
A woman of equal charm, except Quduro
Whose fairness is famed throughout the entire land.

Consider how Baar appears in her richest garb,
With finely polished slippers of soft wood,
(7) Rare leather amulets, and silken scarf.
Necklace of amber, blue and scarlet robes,
And silver rings that glow with amethysts.
When she is clad like this, and sits near me,
I look at her from the corner of my eyes,
And want to see no other thing on earth,
So deep my happiness at seeing her.

But comeliness is not her only gift –
Her strong hands weave the mats and tend the fire;
Swiftly she works, with every task well done.
She is the one who gives her parents pride,
She is dear to them—ah, yes and expensive, too !
For her sake, one whole family I destroyed--
That is to say, when I divorced my wife
(8) And broke our dwelling-place, to marry Baar.
She is the one whose tribe is great in strength,
Generous to strangers, wise among themselves.

She is the one who, in her youth, was blessed
By God's goodwill, and grew more favoured far
Than any other woman of her tribe.
She is the one who scorns the stealthy thief
That goes by night to take the naked woman.
She is the one whose family Allah aids,
Only because they are the kin of Baar.

(9) To all the tribes of Harti and Ishaak,
To men of Jaarti, Absame, Geri, Esa,
And even to the far Audal of Zeilah,
Baar, I tell you, is like the sun itself.
When you behold my lovely, incomparable Baar,
Your own wives, in your eyes, will all be old.
Alas, alas, for ye who hear my song!

NOTES ON "QARAAMI"

(1) This gabei was written about 1937, by a young
Aidagalleh poet named Elmi "Bonderii", who is now dead.
The "Bonderii" is a nick-name, but he was so well known
by it that I have been unable to find out his surname. It
is an odd name, as it is sometimes called "Boderii", both
being corruptions of the English words "boundary" and
"border". Elmi Bonderii was born in the country close to
the Ethiopian border, and was therefore given the name of
Elmi the Borderman.

According to information received from Hersi Jama,
Elmi Bonderii never married at all. The chief and tragic
love affair in his life was not with a woman named Baar.

Elmi worked in a tea shop in the Berbera 'magala'. He
was a handsome lad, but he did not have much money, and
his family had only a few camels. One day he saw a
beautiful girl about fifteen years old, named Hodan Abdill-
lahi. Her tribe was Habr Yunis, Musa Arreh. Bonderii
fell in love with her. He tried to get her tribe to agree to
his marrying her, but the tribe refused because the young
man was so poor. Ultimately, Hodan was married to one
Mohamed Shabel (Mohamed the Leopard). But Bonderii
continued to love her, and cherished his hopeless passion for

five or six years. Then, I am told, "He died of love. Nothing else." Apparently, when Bonderii was on his death-bed, he sent word to Hodan, and asked if she would come to see him. She did come, and stood beside his bed, weeping. As he looked up and saw her, the story goes, he cried aloud and sank back, dead.

Although it has been, of course, dramatized to some extent, the facts of his life seem fairly certain until the death-bed scene. As for his death, every Somali I have talked to about the matter believes implicitly that Bonderii really did die of love, and who am I to say he did not? He was thirty-five years old when he died, and had composed many gabei, all of them on the theme of love.

It is possible that, since Hodan was already married, Bonderii could not use her name in poetry, and so used the name "Baar" in "Qaraami", and included other fictional circumstances, to prevent the wrath of Mohamed Shabel from being directed towards him.

(2) "Her fine-shaped bones . . " Literally, "her joints are tender and flexible, and her bones stand out distinctly under the flesh."

(3) "Magnificent of bearing", "A proud grace", etc. Here, as in many other Somali poems, great value is placed upon good carriage and a graceful walk.

(4) "Her gums' dark gloss" . . Dark shining gums are a mark of beauty.

(5) "Some malicious djinn" . . Djinn are spirits, some good and some evil. An insane person is said to be possessed by djinn.

(6) Qaabiil and Haabiil are the Arabic names for Cain and Abel. There is a legend that Cain and Abel fought over a woman, and both were killed. However, elsewhere in Somali poetry, Cain is said to have killed Abel out of jealousy and pride (see gabei on "Pride").

(7) "Rare leather amulets" . . These would contain special blessings from the Qoran, written on a slip of paper and sealed into the small leather case. These amulets are worn around the neck or on the wrist.

(8) "And broke our dwelling-place" . . When a man divorces his wife and marries another woman, the original "akhal" or grass hut is not used for the dwelling-place of the second marriage. The original family settlement is either deserted and a new one built, or, in some cases, the hut is literally-broken up and destroyed.

(9) "All the tribes . ." Bonderii has listed the main tribes of Ishaak and Darod, the two great sections of the Somali people. It is a complicated way of saying that everyone in the land admires Baar.

III. SOMALI PROSE

TRANSLATED STORIES

1. 'IGAAL BOWKAHH

'Igaal Bowkahh was the name he went by. He was a wizened little thing, with one crippled leg, and by no means handsome to look upon.

One time 'Igaal Bowkahh decided to journey far away from the 'akhals' of his tribe, in order to get work and send home money to his family. After much travelling and many hardships, he found himself in the country of South Africa.

One day, in a town called Johannesburg, 'Igaal Bowkahh was seized by a wild and reckless desire for gaiety and good food and the laughter of companions. And so, within the space of a single day and night he had flung away every rupee of his savings. But 'Igaal did not mourn for his lost wealth. He was not that sort of man. Immediately, he began making new plans, and very soon he decided to go to another town, which was a distance of four nights away. In his pockets only seven guineas remained. How was he to travel?

In those days, there were no railways and no airplanes, and any man who wanted to travel to a far-distant place had to hire slaves or coolies to carry him in a strange contraption called a hammock. But 'Igaal did not travel in this grand style. Having only seven guineas to his name, he was forced to.set out on foot. The coolies who carried people in hammocks charged a great deal of money for their services, and they haughtily refused poor 'Igaal's seven guineas. But he was a stout-hearted man, and set out cheerily, walking at a good pace despite his crippled leg.

Along the road he chanced to meet a man leading a fine shaggy-coated dog, which was for sale.

"Now, my good 'Igaal," said he to himself, "may God permit you to buy this animal and re-sell it at a handsome profit in some neighbouring village."

So he offered the man seven guineas for the dog, which the man accepted gladly.

Then, with no money at all in his pockets, 'Igaal Bowkahh travelled for a short time with the dog, feeling very proud of himself for his good bargain, since dogs were expensive in that country. As he was walking along, however, he suddenly felt he would like a cigar. Not one single cigar did he have with him. Ordinarily, he smoked a good deal, and now, as he thought of a cigar, the desire for one became stronger and stronger.

Finally, arriving at a village, he made up his mind, and forthwith he sold the seven-guinea dog for one cigar, and continued on his way in good spirits.

Just before the time of evening prayers, 'Igaal came to another small settlement. By this time he was faint and bleary-eyed from lack of food and water. There was no one in the village to whom he could go for help, and he felt very lonely and desolate.

However, he made the best of a bad lot, and settled himself as comfortably as possible in a sheltered little valley near the town.

Now the village had many donkeys, and every day they were used for ploughing, but at night they grazed till dawn in the valley near the settlement. As it happened, they were grazing close to the place where 'Igaal was now trying to sleep and forget the hunger that tore at him.

As he sat quietly under the trees, 'Igaal saw the donkeys. For a long while he regarded them with considerable interest. Among the donkeys there was a big mule, and 'Igaal gazed reflectively at the sturdy fellow.

While he stared at the mule and the donkeys, the moon rose and flooded the valley with soft light. It was the fifteenth night of the moon, by the order of God.

'Igaal began to have memories of home. He thought with nostalgia of the Somalis, and how they used to attack and loot each other's camel herds.

"Well, now, why not?" said he to himself, looking again at the donkeys.

Then, like a true man of action, 'Igaal rose and wrapped his cotton robe around his waist, in preparation for riding. He lost no time in cutting with his knife the ropes which tied the donkeys. Craftily, he caught the mule with a bridle and halted the animal near a large stone. Since he was a tiny man, he climbed the stone and from there mounted the mule.

'Igaal gathered up his strength, then, and kicked the mule four times near the big vein along its belly. The mule bellowed in pain, and galloped away at an incredible speed, and the confused donkeys followed. Then 'Igaal flapped his arms like a bird and howled like a hyena, and the donkeys, terrified by this time, ran along in front of him, taking the familiar road which led to the fields.

Hearing all this uproar, the people of the village, alarmed and frightened, came running out of their houses to see what had happened. But what could they do? They could not reach the stampeding donkeys on foot. And so they watched helplessly, returning at last in chagrin to their houses.

Igaal drove and drove and drove all night. When the dawn came, he reached a village which would be two nights away to a traveller on foot. Straightaway, 'Igaal took the donkeys to the market-place. In that town, dogs and donkeys and mules fetched a good price. It is natural that these animals should be so expensive in that country, as the people are a poor lot who do not keep camels. 'Igaal, therefore, got the immense sum of thirty guineas, on an average, for each donkey.

And thus the man who had been poverty-stricken five minutes before, now found himself with bulging pockets. His grand manner returned speedily to 'Igaal. He could not be bothered waiting for all the money to be paid to him, but when most of it was in his possession he mounted his mule and went to the village shops, where he gorged himself with food. Then he set out gaily on his mule to reach his destination.

When he drew close to a place called Durban, he got off his mule.

"All right, my friend," he said to the animal, "You have served me well. Now you may go home."

And he briskly slapped the mule and sent it off.

He entered the 'magala', sauntering along casually, and when he was passing the market-place, he heard a group of men speaking Somali.

One of them was saying,

" . . . and the troops took my camels, and the Dervishes were after me, and I would have been killed were it not for . . . "

'Igaal was astonished. He turned to the man.

"Ma nabad ba!" he cried, "Is it peace? How goes life with you?"

It was the turn of the men to be surprised, since they had never expected to see another Somali in Durban.

"It is peace!" they returned. "Are you a Somali, then?"

"Of course, I am," 'Igaal answered.

"Well, think of that!" they cried, "And where did you come from?"

As 'Igaal Bowkahh thought of his adventures, he began to swell with pride, and before long he was telling the other Somalis the whole tale. Then he asked them for news about themselves.

"We are firemen on a ship," they answered.

"Aha! And could I find a job on that ship, do you think?" he asked.

"It's quite possible," they said, "If you like, we'll take you to the captain, and you can ask him about it."

So 'Igaal found himself before the ship's captain, who looked him over and decided to put him on the crew list.

The ship sailed that night, and 'Igaal with it. And so it was that the man who had done so much evil found himself in a safe refuge, and as he worked he felt his soul had entered into peace.

Ultimately, 'Igaal Bowkahh came with the ship to Aden. When he had disembarked and was drinking tea in the town, he began to tell his story to some young Somalis of his tribe who were working in Aden.

When he had finished, they looked at him wryly.

"To tell the truth," they commented, "We think you must have been mad."

"And why?" asked 'Igaal indignantly.

"Well, why did you give seven guineas for a dog?" they inquired, "And why did you give the dog away for one cigar? These are surely the actions of a man whose mind is unbalanced."

'Igaal Bowkahh laughed.

"You are small children," he said in scorn, "I don't know why I bother to talk to you at all."

"What do you mean?" they asked.

"Well," 'Igaal said, "if you saw the world falling down, what could you do, by yourself, to put it right again?"

"Obviously there is nothing anyone could do," the young men replied.

'Igaal smiled at them.

"Look here," he said. "The best thing to do in that situation is to give the world a good hard kick and make it topple over properly! When I saw that my fortune was at a low ebb, I thought I might as well give it a shove and finish it off. But it turned out well for me, because, as the proverb says, 'A hard stomach is the personal friend of God.' "

2. THE STRANGE AND TERRIBLE CAMEL

(*NOTE*: In Somali, this amusing fantasy is in the Benadir dialect, a dialect which is considered to be humorous. This story is a good example of a type of humour, common in Somali literature, in which things of a highly fantastic nature are taken completely for granted, indeed, treated in as casual a method as possible.)

It was a big town, and formerly it had been heavily populated. But inside the town there lived a gigantic camel, a strange and terrible camel, who ate humans. No one in the town could escape, because the camel never left the town, not even for a single moment. More and more people disappeared into the camel's jaws, until there was no one left in the town at all, and the evil camel reigned alone.

Of all the townsfolk, only one man and his wife and their old woman-servant remained uneaten. Their house was down under the earth, and they lived there in the darkness like animals, eating roots and barely managing to live.

At last the man could stand this cave life no longer.

"I am going out into the open today," he said to his wife.

The woman caught at his shoulders in alarm.

"Don't go outside our cavern!" she pleaded. "The camel will eat you! This is a cruel existence, but at least it is life."

But the man refused to listen to her advice. He went out into the open, and sure enough, the fierce camel found him and ate him.

Now the woman was carrying a child in her womb, and when her husband did not return, she wept and cried, both for herself and for her unborn child. And the old woman wept also.

Four months later, the woman gave birth to a son.

The years passed, and the baby became a lad. He was very good at fashioning toys for himself, and one day he made an arrow, stripping a piece of branch, and whittling it down until it was sharp and pointed.

With the arrow he sometimes killed small animals. Then he would bring these to his mother.

"Mother," he would ask, "is this the one that killed my father?"

"No," his mother would say, "it was a camel that ate your poor father. It is a gigantic and terrible camel. You can never kill it, my son. Leave it alone."

But the boy was not satisfied.

"I made a vow," he would reply, "that I would kill that animal, and kill it I will. You wait and see."

One day, the boy made preparations for going above the earth into the open.

"Mother," he said, "if I don't return after one day, consider me lost. For I am going out from our cavern. And, oh my mother, I wish you to do something for me. Will you go and cook a great deal of food for me to take on my journey?"

His mother sighed, but as she saw the boy was determined, she agreed.

"This food you want," she said. "What is it and how do I make it?"

"The camel that I am going to kill," the boy explained, "has been very wicked. In its belly there are many people. They are alive there, and it is they who will eat the food, for they will be hungry after all this time inside the camel."

"Very well," the mother replied, "It shall be as you say."

When the boy had made all his preparations, he said farewell to his mother.

" Go, my son," his mother said, "And may God be with you."

And so the boy went up out of the cavern, and walked through the deserted streets of the town. Finally, he came to the camel, which was more hideous and more terrible than he had ever imagined.

The boy hid himself behind a tree. Then he knelt, and grasped his bow, and took aim, and shot one arrow.

The camel shrieked with pain, and in a deep gruff voice it spoke.

"The bush country here is without people and without animals, and yet I swear it has a very good aim!"

Then the boy took another arrow, and shot it, and hit the camel in the kidney. The great beast moaned and roared, and then it spoke again in its deep gruff voice.

"This bush country has no people and no animals," the camel cried. "But by all the saints, its aim is good!"

Then the boy shot another arrow, and the third arrow hit the camel in the mouth. Then the strange animal spoke no more, but fell down dead.

As soon as the camel had fallen, the boy rose and ran over to it. With a sharp knife, he cut open the gigantic camel's gigantic stomach.

Then all the people who were inside the camel's belly came running out, singing for joy.

But as it happened, when the boy was cutting open the camel, his knife had injured his uncle.

The other people took the boy up on their shoulders, and praised him and called him a warrior and a hero.

But his uncle was very angry.

"My own nephew has injured me with his knife! What impudence is this! I will teach him to be more respectful!"

The people begged the uncle not to be angry, but he insisted that he would fight his nephew.

He took an arrow and came up to the small boy.

"Now then, take this," he said, "and get ready to fight me. No man injures me and escapes."

"Uncle," the boy said humbly, "I did not mean to hurt you with my knife. Please forgive me."

But his ill-tempered uncle refused.

"No forgiveness will you get from me," he said. "Here . . . take this arrow, and go and stand there. I will stand here."

And so it was arranged. The uncle shot at the boy, but the arrow missed. Then the man said to his nephew.

"All right—you shoot now."

The boy shot the arrow, and hit his uncle in the gullet. Then the uncle fell down and died, and all the people buried him.

And as for the brave lad, he became the Sultan of that country.

3. How the Meat was Divided

It is said that once, long ago, all the beasts of prey went hunting together, and killed a she-camel. Then they gathered around to divide the meat among them, into thirty-two equal parts, according to the custom of the Somalis. And each animal waited to receive his portion. Then the great-maned lion spoke.

"Omar the hyena, you shall divide the meat," he said.

And so the hyena came forward to divide the meat, half and half, quarter and quarter, according to the custom of our people.

"Now then," the hyena began, "Half and half. One half will go to the lion, and the other half to the rest of the animals for your further division by agreement."

Then the mighty lion became angry, and glared furiously at the hyena.

"This is the worst meat division I have ever seen!" the lion cried.

And he gave the hyena a powerful blow with his paw, so that the poor beast's eye was torn out of its socket.

Omar the hyena whimpered with pain, and crawled away. Then the lion turned to the other animals, who cowered before him. Finally he called in a regal fashion for the she-jackal.

"Omar the hyena did not know how to divide the meat properly," the lion said. "Nia(1) You, Mother Jackal, let us see if you are wiser in meat division."

And so the jackal came forward to divide the meat, half and half, quarter and quarter, according to the custom of our people.

"Very well," said she. "Half and half. Half the meat belongs to the lordly lion. The other half, quarter and quarter. One quarter goes to the mighty lion. The other quarter, eighth and eighth. One eighth goes to the fearless lion. The other eighth, sixteenth and sixteenth. One sixteenth goes to the noble lion. The other sixteenth, thirty-secondth and thirty-secondth. One thirty-secondth goes to the brave lion. The other thirty-secondth belongs to all you other animals, for your further peaceful division."

At this the lion threw back his head and laughed.

"Well, Mother Jackal," he said, "I see you know how to divide meat properly. Who taught you such wise division?"

The she-jackal smiled.

"What taught me this wise division," she replied softly, "was the eye of Omar the hyena, which I saw hanging from its socket."

NOTE :

(1) "Nia" is the Somali word for calling a woman, "Waria" being used to call a man. Both correspond roughly to "Hey!"

4. RIGHT AND WRONG

Once an old man gave some advice to his young son.

"My boy," he said, "whatever you do in this world people will not be satisfied with it. That is the way of people."

But the boy, being very young and inexperienced, would not believe him.

"Very well," the father said. "Let us take the donkey and go into the town. Perhaps I can show you there the truth of my words."

So they took the donkey and began leading it along the road.

And people looked at them queerly, and began whispering:

"What a silly man—leading a donkey, and walking himself. He must be a fool."

At this, the boy grew very upset.

"They are saying we are fools," he said. "Please get on the donkey, father, before any more people see us travelling this way and think we are mad."

So the old man got on the donkey, and they continued on their way.

But soon they heard people talking about them again.

"What a dreadful old man," the people said. "Riding on the donkey, and making such a small boy walk. He must be a cruel father."

At this, the boy grew worried.

"The people are saying terrible things about you, my father," he said. "So perhaps it would be better if I rode the donkey and you walked."

And they did so. But soon people began whispering about them once more.

"What a dreadful young boy," they said, "riding on the donkey and letting his old father walk. Ah, but the young are getting selfish these days!"

So the boy suggested to his father that they both mount the donkey.

After a few minutes, however, again they heard the scornful voices.

"What unkind people—two of them sitting on one tiny donkey! Such people do not deserve to own animals."

And the old man smiled at his son.

"You see?" he said, "You must do what you think is best, and not worry what people will say."

5. LEGEND OF THE 'JINNA' OR STINK-ANT

If you go to the 'jinna' and ask him why he is so thin in the waist, he will explain thus,

"It is a result of riding a great deal on a fine horse. Anyone knows that riding draws a man in at the waist."

And if you ask him why he smells so badly, he will answer,

"Because I once visited a woman who had a stinking birth."

And if you ask him why his jaws are open so wide, the 'jinna' will explain,

"Because I used to go with a group of boys from village to village, dancing, and I was the one who went in front, shouting that we did not come to beg food or money, but only came to dance."

Thus would the 'jinna' speak if you asked him.

6. THE MAN WHO HAD FOUR WIVES

Once there was a man who had four wives. All were good women, but unfortunately each was jealous of the others, and they were forever squabbling.

One day they came to him and said they would like to ask him one question.

"Tell us which one of us you love most," they demanded.

The man pondered for a moment, and then he called all the four to him.

"Your question will be answered," he said. "I shall touch the one I love the best. Close your eyes."

And they did so. And the man, in his wisdom, touched all four of them.

"There now," he said, "I have touched the one I love the most."

The four women opened their eyes and smiled at one another. And henceforth there was peace in that house.

7. HIGH OR LOW

(NOTE : There is a Somali proverb, "Whether the spear be held high or low, it is well." This is supposed to be the story from which the proverb grew.)

It is said that once a very clever man ruled as Sultan of all this land. Disputes and quarrels were brought to him, and with his wit and good sense he could always settle them.

One day a cow got into a garden and ate most of it. Then the man who owned the garden complained to the Sultan. The Sultan therefore made a decree ordering any man who owned a cow that grazed in another man's garden to give the owner of the garden a pile of jowari as high as his spear reached.

Some time later, it happened that one of the Sultan's cows grazed in another man's garden. All the people laughed at the Sultan's predicament.

"Today your cow grazed in another man's garden," they said to him, "And you must pay the price, according to your own decree."

"Quite true," said the clever Sultan. "This much jowari will I pay, a pile as tall as my spear when it lies on the earth. The decree did not state which way the spear must be!"

8. THE CHEATING LESSON

"Uncle," said a small boy to a man of his tribe, "I have a request to make. I would like you to teach me how to cheat, that I may earn my living easily from fools."

The man considered for a moment, and then he turned to the boy and smiled.

"Very well," he replied, "I will teach you, if this morning you will let me milk the she-camel which you have been milking these past days. Later I will give you the first lesson."

"All right," the boy said, "I agree."

And so it happened that the man milked the she-camel that day, and the boy went without milk, according to their agreement. Then the boy grew impatient, and spoke to the man again.

"Now teach me cheating," he begged.

The man patter the boy on the head and smiled at him.

"I have done so already," he replied, "For this morning I milked your camel, little one, and you went without milk."

9. THE TOWNSMAN

It happened that a Somali who had been brought up in Cardiff came back home to Somaliland one year. He knew nothing about camels and the ways of camel-tending, nor did he have any knowledge of the herders' life. He had lived in a large city since his childhood. When he reached Somaliland, however, he bought some camels and sheep and went out into the Haud with them.

One day he was driving his camels along, when a small camel ran up and bit him. The man was very angry, and so he hit the young camel with a stick.

Almost at once, a big camel who was the mother of the baby one, came rushing up and began to attack the man.

"Wait a minute!" shouted the unfortunate townsman to the mother camel, "Inspector, he bit me first!"

10. THE BLIND SHEIKH

(NOTE : This is considered by Somalis to be an extremely humorous story.)

There once was an old sheikh, who was blind, and he was famed throughout the country for his wonderful wisdom. One day a group of people gathered to talk with him.

"Good people," the blind sheikh said, "I beg you to tell me the name of this strange object that I touch with my hand."

And he reached out and touched an anthill.

"It is an anthill, oh wise sheikh," the people replied.

"Do you say so?" the sheikh commented mildly. "That is most interesting to me. It is so very large, this hill. It is a wonder of wonders. It is a great great wonder."

Then the people told him that it was made by an insect called 'abor', and was very cunningly constructed from the termite's saliva and from sand.

"Indeed?" said the sheikh. "Well, this is a wonder of wonders, to be sure."

And then they told him that 'abor' makes the hill only at night. The old sheikh shook his head in astonishment.

"Is that the way it is?" he replied. "Indeed, this is really a great wonder, the greatest of great wonders."

PARAPHRASED STORIES

A. TALES ARABIC IN ORIGIN

1. AHMED THE WOODSELLER

One time, many years and hundreds of years ago, there lived in the city of Sennah in the Yemen, an insignificant little man called Ahmed Hatab, or Ahmed the Woodseller. He was not greatly blessed by fate, having a squat ugly countenance and a shrunken and twisted body. He had a wife, but she could not be called a blessing, being a large shrewish creature who nagged at Ahmed because he was so poor.

And indeed, Ahmed Hatab must have been the poorest man in all Arabia, at least among those who had an ostensible means of livelihood. Ahmed the Woodseller would go out every morning, just before dawn, to the bush-land and plains, in order to gather firewood. In the evening, he would drive his little donkey-cart through the streets of the town, selling the wood he had gathered.

And every day, from the sale of his firewood, Ahmed Hatab made three annas. Only three little annas. Never any less, but never any more either. He might try as hard as he could to gather more wood, and he might shout the praises of his warped twigs at the top of his voice, but three annas was the sum he always made.

Now this, it will readily be seen, was no life for a man, especially a man of Ahmed's talents. For in spite of his wizened frame and his small blinking eyes, Ahmed rather fancied himself as a clever man and a philosopher, and would sometimes boast of how well he would have run the country, had he only been fortunate enough to be born a Sultan.

But despite his wonderful day-dreams, Ahmed never got anywhere. He did not make enough money to feed himself and his wife, much less to save anything towards the silk merchant's business for which he longed. There was never enough food in the house for the two of them. And his wife was constantly complaining and telling him that she might have married Suleban, the silver merchant, although, as a matter of fact, this was not true. Ahmed grew more and more weary with his life, and took to pondering on it while he collected his chips of firewood in the country.

"Ahmed, you are a fool," he said to himself one day. "And may Allah bear witness to your stupidity. Here you spend years' slaving to collect firewood, and what does it profit you? What does the pale fire of sunrise, or the cool dawn, or the singing of birds mean to you? Only another day to scrabble among the thorn-bushes, picking up bits of stick. Why toil thus, to make three miserable annas a day? Better to die now, and get it over quickly, than to struggle and suffer, and die of starvation in the end."

And so it was that Ahmed Hatab determined to kill himself.

The next morning, therefore, instead of setting out for the bush to collect his wood, Ahmed girded his brown rag of a robe around his waist, and marched off towards a very steep mountain beyond the city.

Never had the dawn been so sweet, or the voices of the birds so clear. But Ahmed would not turn back.

The mountain was high indeed, and Ahmed puffed and staggered over broken rocks and shale, climbing to the top. But thin and underfed as he was, ultimately his determination won out, and he arrived at the mountain's peak, dazed and exhausted.

At the top of the mountain there was a craggy precipice which dropped down thousands of feet and ended in a mass of sharp-pointed rocks. Ahmed, trembling a little, sauntered up to the edge of this cliff.

"World," he said, wiping away the odd tear that had come into his eyes, "Now you lose a man who might have been a prince, a philosopher or a poet. A man who might have sung songs that would make the shy lovely women unveil their faces, and the urchins in the street turn gentle and wondering. But fate made him a gatherer of faggots, and so . . ."

He broke off suddenly. He had heard a footstep behind him. Who would be so mad, he wondered, as to climb this mountain? Ahmed turned around.

There, standing behind him, was a tall man with fine sharp features and kindly eyes.

Now this' stranger, unknown to Ahmed Hatab, was none other than Nebii Hhudur, the good prophet who travels the world disguised as a beggar.

" Friend," Nebii Hhudur said quietly, " What are you doing, standing in this perilous place?"

Ahmed glared angrily at him.

"Why should the curiosity of strangers be rewarded with the trust of friendship?" he demanded.

" I am not a stranger, Ahmed Hatab," Hhudur replied, "And your fate concerns me more than you think."

"Well, since you must know," Ahmed replied, secretly rather pleased to tell his story to someone. "The truth is that I am going to kill myself. I am a miserable wood-seller who has never in his life made more than three annas a day. Three annas a day is not sufficient to keep even a child, much less a hard-working man like myself, and my grasping greedy wife, who, I may say, eats more than twenty camels. Therefore I have determined to put an end to this nonsense called life."

Nebii Hhudur nodded understandingly.

"I realize," he said, "That your position has been a hard one. But will you not reconsider, Ahmed? Will you not go back? You have been a good man, worshipping

Allah and doing kindness to others. Perhaps your fortune is on the point of changing, and you will arrive back at your house to find wealth waiting for you.

But Ahmed only laughed bitterly.

Wallahi, Billahi, Tallahi!" he cried, "You have mistaken me for a child, to babble pretty stories at me in this fashion! No. For many years I hoped, and now hope is at an end."

Hhudur shrugged his shoulders.

"Very well," he said, "Go ahead and jump. But I should warn you—your time is not yet up, and this you will presently learn."

And when Ahmed Hatab glanced up, the other man had vanished as though he had never stood there.

Ahmed scratched his head under the flimsy turban he wore.

"This is most odd," he said to himself. "There was a man talking to me, and pleasantly, too, in this very spot, and now he has disappeared. Well, it may be I am lightheaded from want of food, and was merely talking to myself."

And so, with all the vigour he could command, Ahmed Hatab turned again to the cliff and jumped off into space.

Thousands of feet he fell, through the air, past the thorn trees on the mountain's rim and the rocks that jutted out menacingly. When he looked towards the bottom of the ravine and saw the pointed teeth of the rocks below, Ahmed shuddered in every limb with a terrible fear, and closed his eyes.

Crash! He had landed at the bottom. He lay there, perhaps for half an hour, quite still and motionless.

Then he discovered that he could still think.

"I am dead," he thought, "I must be dead. But what happens now, in God's name? Where are the gardens, and the fountains, and the soft green couches that the Kitab promises?"

Then, moving himself gently, he stubbed his toe against a sharp rock, and shouted in pain.

He was not dead after all, but very much alive.

He sat up and stared at the mountain, and felt his limbs all over, and scratched his ill-shapen head.

"But this is wondrous strange!" he cried, "Here am I and there is the mountain, and certainly, I was at the top a few minutes ago, and now am here, at the bottom. And most certainly I have not grown wings. How is it that I am unhurt?"

And he stared at the mountain again.

Then Ahmed Hatab grew angry, and fury shook his small body.

"Cheated!" he gasped, "I have been cheated! Some devil has played a trick on me! But I have determined to die, and by all the saints and djinn, I will die!"

And he rose, and clambered manfully over the broken rock until he came to a large thorn thicket.

Now these thorn bushes had needles as long as a man's middle finger, and their points were sharper than a Sultan's sword.

Ahmed smiled gleefully to himself as he looked at the thicket.

"Very well," he said, "Now we shall see!"

And he dived head-first into the bushes.

But strange to tell, he emerged the other side, and when he had picked himself up, he realized that he had not even so much as a single scratch upon his body.

Then Ahmed the Woodseller grew very angry indeed, and swore by all the saints and djinn, and by the Prophet's beard, that he would die, and die before the sun set that very day.

And so it happened that he walked over the dusty roads and through the scorching sand, until he came to the shore of the turquoise sea.

"Now, let us see who will die and who will live," he said to himself in triumph, "They will hear of my death in the city, and they will say, 'Poor Ahmed Hatab—he has drowned himself, in a most horrible fashion, and the fishes have chewed his bones. Why did we not help him when he was alive?' Thus they will speak, and my wife (may she eat stones!) will be desolate. Oh sea, Ahmed Hatab comes to you this day!"

And so, with a great flourish of his short arms, Ahmed plunged into the sea, and began splashing through the water in his haste to get out beyond his depth.

But the further he went, the further the water seemed to retreat, and when he had splashed along for a mile or more, the sea was still not above his skinny ankles.

Ahmed Hatab stood still and looked at the land. It was a long way off now, and the gentle waves were lapping around his toes.

Then an enormous discouragement took possession of him, and slowly he plodded back to shore.

He walked along the road again, and took the turning that led into the city, still pondering his bad luck and wondering how he could kill himself.

"The mountain is no good," he said to himself despondently, "The thorns are no good. And finally, the sea itself refused to have me. Is it possible that I shall have to go back again to hauling wood for three disgusting annas a day, and live with that poisonous-tongued woman? Never! Never! Ah, Ahmed Hatab, your brains must be called upon to work quickly!"

As he wandered along the road, musing in this fashion, he saw something lying in the dust. When he got closer, he perceived that it was a dead man. The fortunate fellow had evidently been murdered by thieves, since his purse was gone, and his head knocked in, and a blood-stained club lay beside him.

Ahmed looked at the dead man for a long time. And then a gleam of light came into his eyes. He picked up the club, and fondled it, and sat down to wait.

Finally, as he had anticipated, the Sultan's soldiers came along the road.

Ahmed Hatab smiled winningly at them, and flourished the club.

"Salaam aleikum!" he shouted, "I have killed this man!"

The soldiers regarded him coldly.

"You are obviously mad," they said, "To sit by the corpse and to shout out your guilt so readily. But if you have killed him, then you shall be killed yourself for your crime, according to the law, madman or not."

And so they took Ahmed back to the Sultan's palace with them, and brought him before the Sultan, who commanded them to cut off the head of the little woodseller.

"Ah, now the time has come at last!" Ahmed whispered to himself, with nervous elation. "Nothing can stop your death now, my good Ahmed!"

The soldiers took him out to the prison courtyard and put his head on a block, and the executioner came up with a huge scimitar in his hand.

"You are indeed a queer one," the executioner said, "To be grinning and smiling just before my sharp friend has made its acquaintance with your neck. But queer or not, the Sultan has said your head should be severed from your body, and severed it will be."

And with these words, the executioner, who was a stout strong man, brought the scimitar down on the scrawny neck of Ahmed Hatab.

But then a wonderful thing happened. The blade of the scimitar, tempered steel as it was, shattered into a thousand pieces, and the neck of Ahmed Hatab remained unscathed.

The soldiers cried out in amazement and fear, and the executioner shouted in anger.

"This blade is faulty!" he cried, "I have never seen such a thing before! Bring me another scimitar, and a stronger one, of flawless steel!"

And thus it was done. But again the scimitar broke, and Ahmed's neck did not. A third time a new blade was brought, and a third time the steel gave way beneath that seemingly tender neck.

Then the executioner grew frightened. He wiped the sweat from his face, and trembled visibly.

"It is a miracle," he whispered. "Take this man back. to the Sultan, for I will not touch him again!"

"No!" cried Ahmed, in anguish, "I beg you, worthy executioner, to try once more! Perhaps all the blades were faulty. Perhaps you did not swing the scimitar properly."

"I always swing the blade properly," the executioner said, rather testily, "No, I am sorry, friend, since you seem to want to die, but I shall have nothing further to do with you."

Then Ahmed broke out into loud wailing and sobbing, and the assembled company shook their heads and clicked their tongues, and said he was quite mad.

But when the Sultan heard of the unusual occurrence, he turned pale.

"Let the man go free," the Sultan said, "For I would not meddle with one whom God intends to let live."

And so it happened that Ahmed Hatab, still alive and still penniless, was turned free again.

Aimlessly, he wandered through the streets of the city, and his wanderings took him to the city walls. When he got there, he thought he would walk to the next town, some miles away, and try his luck at dying there.

"This city of Sennah," he told himself grimly, "Has always been against me. First the three annas, and now this. Was ever a man so unfortunate?"

Presently, he came to the next city, and his feet took him to the palace of the Sultan. Now, this Sultan's palace was a rich and splendid building, with many courtyards and fountains and gardens. The whole was guarded most carefully by armed soldiers and by seven massive dogs with long sharp teeth and formidable jaws. At each of the seven gateways there were a dozen soldiers with swords, and one fierce dog, all of them ready to kill anyone who attempted to enter.

Little Ahmed Hatab selected a gateway casually, and wandered in through it, dressed in his filthy brown rags. No one stopped him, and indeed, no one appeared to see him at all. This was rather unexpected, so he whistled and sang to draw attention to himself. But the guards still stood stiffly beside the gate as though he were not there, and the watch-dog did not even look up.

So Ahmed got angry again, and stamped into the palace itself, through long corridors hung with rich carpets, and into the throne-room of the great Sultan.

The Sultan, as it happened, was sitting in his throne-room with all his advisers and wise-men. As the door opened, and ragged Ahmed marched in, they all looked up in astonishment. The wise men and elders jumped to their feet, horrified. One or two of the noble gentlemen, under the impression that Ahmed was a dangerous assassin, hid themselves under the carpets. The rest shouted for guards. Only the Sultan did not make a huge fuss.

"Well, now," the Sultan said, a certain surprise showing in his aristocratic features, "Who are you, my good man, and how in the name of all the saints did you get in here?"

"May God preserve your Mightiness, oh Pearl of Sultans," Ahmed replied humbly, "I walked in."

"What?" cried the Sultan, "With all my armed guards and my seven ferocious watch-dogs at the gates?"

"Indeed," said Ahmed, "That is how it happened."

"You are a curious fellow," the Sultan said. "But I cannot quite believe you. Go outside my palace once more and try to get in again, and we shall see if my guards and my dogs are so blind and lazy twice."

So Ahmed Hatab took himself outside the palace once more, and for the second time he wandered in through the gates. And neither the guards nor the watch-dogs stirred.

Then it came about that the Sultan of that city was vastly amused, and admired Ahmed Hatab for his supposed cleverness in slipping past the guards. So he decided to make Ahmed one of his advisers, and to bestow an estate on him, and to give him one of the royal princesses as a wife.

The Sultan's youngest daughter was a lovely girl, slim and bright-eyed, and graceful as a flower. She came and combed the beard of Ahmed Hatab, and gave him fine clothes of embroidered brocades and spoke to him most gently and lovingly. Ahmed had never seen such a woman in all his life, and his heart flamed with love and desire for her.

In a few days, the daughter of the Sultan was married to the little woodseller, who was now grown very grand, with his neatly trimmed beard and the rich clothes that almost hid his malformed body.

So it was that Ahmed Hatab, having found good fortune far beyond his dreams, decided that life was after all worth living.

"Now I shall not die," said he, "For, truly, life has turned marvellously prosperous for me. At last I have achieved that wealth so long denied me, and I will live until I am an old greybeard, and will grow more mighty and more rich every year. To say nothing of happiness— ah, what a jewel the girl is! Ahmed, at last the life you deserve has come to you!"

But at that moment, a faint breeze came in through the window, and when Ahmed looked around, there stood an angel, staring at him.

"By the Prophet (on whose Name be Peace!)," cried Ahmed in fear, "To what do I owe this visit?"

"I am sorry," the angel said quietly, "But your life is over now, Ahmed Hatab. It is your time to die, and I have been sent for you."

Then Ahmed grew angry, and waved his arms helplessly, and shouted.

"Ah, the unfairness of it!" he cried bitterly, "Where were you, I ask, when I wanted to die, and jumped off the precipice?"

"Your time had not yet come," the angel said, "And I

had not been ordered to fetch you. But now the hour of death has arrived for you."

Ahmed flung himself, weeping, onto a couch.

"And where," he bellowed, "were you when I leaped into the thorn bush?"

"God had not sent me to fetch you," the angel said. "But now your time of departure from this life has come."

"And where were you," Ahmed sobbed, "When I waded out into the sea, and the water would not come above my ankles, and when the executioner's blade broke, and when the watch-dogs did not flick an eyelash as I entered the Sultan's palace?"

"I have told you," the angel said patiently, "Your time of death was not then. But now it has arrived, and I am here to take you."

Then Ahmed stopped his weeping and moaning, and glanced up with a look of great craftiness.

"Very well," said he, "If I must die, so be it. But you would not have me die, surely, without saying my prayers once more?"

"Why, no," the angel said, "You are free to pray before you die."

"Then," Ahmed said, "Promise me you won't touch me until I have been to the mosque once more."

And so the angel promised, and swore on the Kitab, not to touch Ahmed Hatab until he had visited the mosque once more to pray.

Then Ahmed jumped up joyfully.

"Aha!" he laughed jauntily, "I didn't say when I would go to the mosque, and now, my good friend, I don't intend to go just yet!"

The angel was filled with consternation, and flew back to heaven to complain of the wicked and recalcitrant Ahmed. But when he had told his story, the angel was told to leave Ahmed and to let him continue on his sinful way, for it would not last long, and would profit him nothing.

So the triumphant Ahmed continued to live, and grew more wealthy, and enjoyed his wife, and had a fine house and many servants and much stock. Ultimately he became a well-known Sheikh, and a much-respected adviser of the Sultan.

But he never went inside the mosque.

Then it happened, after several years, that the chief priest of the mosque died, and the Sultan called Ahmed Hatab to him to discuss appointing a new imam.

"You have been my faithful adviser," the Sultan said, "And my son-in-law, and a much-respected man. Now I would like to appoint you as imam at the mosque. It is a great honour, but a great responsibility, also. However, since you have been here, you have studied the Holy writings, and have acquired much knowledge, and I do not doubt that you will fulfil your duties well."

Ahmed trembled with fright. At first, he refused politely, claiming that such an honour was too great for one who had been, after all, born humbly.

But the Sultan insisted. Then Ahmed grew more and more frightened, and refused again and again, beating his forehead with one frenzied hand, and sobbing and jumping about, like a man in a fit.

Then the Sultan's face grew dark with rage.

"Why do you refuse thus?" he demanded.

"Ah, forgive me, Mightiest of all Sultans," Ahmed sobbed miserably, "But if I enter a mosque I shall die, and I am not an old man, and life has a sweet taste!"

"Are you then the offspring of some devil, to fear the holy mosque?" the Sultan asked. "What terrible things are hidden in your mind, Ahmed, my son? No! You shall go to the mosque, and you shall go at once!"

Ahmed protested and wept and struggled, but all in vain. The sturdy guards of the Sultan picked him up bodily, and marched with him to the mosque.

As soon as he was inside the door of the mosque, the angel appeared to Ahmed again.

"Mercy, I beg of you!" cried Ahmed, on his knees

"God is Merciful," the angel said, "Pray to Him."

So Ahmed Hatab, who had tried to cheat death, did not die without saying his final prayers. Then, as he finished praying, he slumped down where he knelt, and the soul departed from the wretched little body of Ahmed the Woodseller.

So do men learn the futility of resisting the commands of Allah, the Compassionate, the Merciful!

2. How Donkeys Came to Be

(NOTE : Nebii (Prophet) Hhudur is the subject of many tales and superstitions in this country. Although these tales are Arabic in origin, they have come to be firmly established in the Somali culture. Hhudur is a man and yet not a man. He is a prophet, although not as great as Abraham, Moses, Jesus or Mohamed. He has been gifted with eternal life. He started life, according to legend, in pre-Islamic times. God has attached certain conditions to Hhudur's gift of eternal life. The prophet must never stay long in the same place, but must wander over the earth, travelling as the wind travels, disappearing and appearing at will, sometimes being carried inside the 'dust-devils', those columns of wind and sand so common in desert countries. He must never marry or settle down. The Somalis believe that Nebii Hhudur often comes to a place in the guise of a beggar. Hhudur prays for those who are kind to him, and they become wealthy. But those who are unkind to him are ruined. No one can tell where Hhudur may be or who he is—he may be the next beggar who approaches one in the town for 'baksheesh'. There is only one way of recognizing Hhudur. In his right thumb there is no bone, only flesh, so that if one shakes hands with him the thumb will bend backwards. There is a belief here that this is the reason why a Muslim will always shake hands by pressing against the thumb of the other person. If anyone finds Hhudur in this way, he is supposed to grasp his hand until his blessing is given, in somewhat the same way as Jacob (Genesis 32 : 26) forced a blessing from the Angel—"I will not let thee go, except thou bless me."

Ahmed Nasir, who told me these tales, claims that a friend of his once saw Nebii Hhudur in Mogadiscio. Ali, the friend, was approached in the street by an old beggar man, who asked him for his hat, since the sun was hot that day. Ali refused, but said that if the old man would come to his house later, he would receive food and clothing. Just then Ahmed came along, and Ali turned to speak to him. When Ali looked around again, there was no old man in sight, only a dust-devil whirling along the street. Ahmed reproached his friend bitterly, saying, "That must have been Nebii Hhudur—you might have been rich tomorrow!")

It happened many years ago that a beggar one day sat crouching beside a dusty road, sick with the fever and chills of malaria, without money or food, and altogether miserable. Also, as the final affliction in a host of afflictions, the wretch's back itched.

Now the fact was that this same beggar was Nebii Hhudur, come to visit the land and pray for the worthy and the generous. But to look at him, he was no different from any other beggar. He wore rags, and filthy rags at that, and his skin was hot and dry with the fever, and his eyes were sore. And as he sat there in his unhappy state, he attempted to reach with his hand around to his back, where the skin itched like a thousand insect bites. But he could not reach the tormenting spot, and his anguish grew by the minute.

Then, along that dusty road there came a band of tribesmen, carrying their few possessions with them, bound for their 'kharia' or tribal camp some miles further on.

"Oh ye Muslims!" cried Nebii Hhudur, "Take pity! I am a poor beggar, with no money and no food!"

The people stared at him coldly.

"We have no money, either," they replied, "And we cannot spare any food. We are taking this jowari and these dates to our kinsmen."

Nebii Hhudur sighed a long sigh. "I have no water, either," he continued, "And I am dry as the desert sand. And furthermore, I am ill with malaria."

"We are sorry," the people answered, with small sympathy. "But we cannot spare any water. We shall thirst, ourselves, before we reach our destination. You will have to fend for yourself, old man."

"Very well," Nebii Hhudur said, "You will not give me food, or money, or even a sip of water. But may I at least ask you to scratch my back, which is plaguing me with its itch?"

But the people only laughed.

"What?" they cried, "Should we break our journey to scratch the back of a filthy beggar? Use the thorns on the branches, old man, for we will not stop!"

With that, they went on their way, and Nebii Hhudur was left beside the road, as miserable as ever.

Presently, another traveller came along the road. This time it was a poorly dressed man, walking by himself, and carrying no water vessels, or food, or possessions of any kind. As he approached Nebii Hhudur, the traveller nodded to him and raised his hand in salute.

"Salaam aleikum, friend," he said. "You look to be in a sorry state, sitting there by the road with no shade trees over you, and the midday sun blazing."

"Aleikum salaam," answered Nebii Hhudur, "You are quite right. I am indeed in a terrible predicament. I am a beggar, and have no money, nor any food or water. My only possession is this malaria, which clings to me like a tick, making me sweat and shiver. And furthermore, cursed by fate as I am, my back itches."

"You are indeed unfortunate," the traveller sympathized. "I cannot give you money, nor any food or water, for as you can see, I have none. I, too, am a poor man. But I can at least scratch your back for you if you wish it."

And so the traveller scratched Nebii Hhudur's back, and the itching which had been plaguing him disappeared.

"Thank you, friend," Nebii Hhudur said. "You have a good heart. And now I shall tell you something. I am no beggar. Nebii Hhudur is my name."

The traveller stared at him.

"Nebii Hhudur! Is it true that you are really Nebii Hhudur?"

"It is true," the other said. "And what is more, God will reward you for your kindness to me. I will pray for you, and before long, you will grow wealthy."

The poor traveller sighed, and glanced shrewdly at the prophet.

" That is all very well," he said. "But how could I become wealthy if I do not have a little money to begin with, some few coins to invest in a business or in camels? I don't suppose you could let me have an advance on the future?"

Nebii Hhudur smiled.

"No," he said, "I have no money. I depend on the generosity of strangers for my livelihood. But do you see those people walking up the road there?"

"Yes, to be sure, a dozen or so of them."

"Well, then, go along and follow them, and when you get close by, shout 'Hurry up, get on there!', and something marvellous will happen."

The traveller thanked Nebii Hhudur and hurried after the people who were plodding along the road.

When he approached them, he began to shout.

"Hurry up! Get on there! Hurry!"

And then, in an instant, before his very eyes, the people had disappeared, and in their place several dozen grey small beasts trotted along the road. They had short

thin legs and round bodies, and enormous ears, and as they
ran through the dust, they brayed in a melancholy fashion.
"Wallahi!" cried the astonished traveller, "What has
happened? It is a miracle! Nothing like these beasts has
ever been seen before! They are partly like horses, but
much smaller. And yet, they look wonderfully strong and
wiry. I wonder . . . "

And he began to think. Surely these little animals
would do very well to carry the water vessels from the
wells, and to pull the woodsellers' and charcoal-vendors'
carts in the town.

So it happened that the traveller herded the animals
into the town, and sold them at a good price to the mer-
chants and woodsellers and town-folk. With the money he
obtained, he himself bought a huge herd of camels, and a
shop, and grew prosperous and wealthy in a few years.

And this was indeed how donkeys came to be born.

3. NEBII HHUDUR AND THE CAMEL BONE

Once there lived a wealthy merchant who loved
nothing so much as gold. Although he had a fine house,
and many servants, and four wives, and a store-house filled
with chests of coin, he was not satisfied. He hankered
after still more riches.

It occurred to him that a good way of obtaining more
wealth would be to lure Nebii Hhudur to a feast, since he
had heard of the fabulous rewards given to those who fed
the good prophet.

So the merchant gave a great feast, and killed many
camels, and fed anyone who came. Each person who came
to his house that day, the merchant scrutinized with his
sharp eyes, wondering if this were Nebii Hhudur. But
all day long, no sign came. People from the town heard
of the feast, and flocked 'to the merchant's house, doing
great justice to the roast camel meat. But Nebii Hhudur
did not come.

At last the merchant grew angry and disgusted.

"I have killed many camels for this feast," he grumbled, "And I have spent a huge amount of money, hoping to make yet more. But here it is nearly dusk, and Nebii Hhudur has not deigned to appear. I have been a fool, wasting my money to give these shiftless people a fine meal!"

At that moment, a strange man came to the door and asked if he might be allowed to enter and share the feast. But the merchant had grown bitter with disappointment.

"Go away!" he shouted. "You are just like all the rest of the gluttons who have eaten all my roast camel meat and will pay me nothing for it. The feast is over! You are too late!"

And so the man walked away. But as he was leaving the merchant's house, one of the servants, a poor lad who worked in the kitchens, came out and greeted him.

"My master has given me only a small portion of the meat for my evening meal," he said, "but you are welcome to share it with me if you have no better fare tonight."

The stranger thanked him, and went with the boy to the small room where the servant lived· There they found the meat, and very little it was, too, a mere shred of flesh on a great hunk of bone.

The servant boy took his knife and carved the meat into two portions, giving one to the stranger. They ate, and when the boy went to throw away the bone, he found it still contained the same amount of meat as before.

"This is strange!" he cried. "But let us not question it, for God has surely seen fit to bless us with more meat. Come, let us share this, also."

They shared the meat, and when they looked at the bone, the same amount of meat still clung to it. Again and again the servant lad carved the meat from the bone, and they ate, and the bone still bore meat.

Then the servant looked at the stranger. The man smiled at him gently. And the boy realized that Nebii

Hhudur had shared his meal with him.

"Do not say a word of this to anyone," Hhudur said, "and soon you will be rewarded."

Then there was a little rush of wind through the bare room, and when the boy looked up, the good prophet had vanished.

Before long, it happened that a Sultan took a liking to the servant lad, and took him into his service, and in a few years he had grown to be the Sultan's chief steward, and was prosperous and respected. But as for the rich man, his shop burned down and his camels withered and grew sick, and his garden suffered a blight, and he ended his life as a beggar in the streets.

4. NEBII HHUDUR AND THE DISH OF JOWARI

Once it happened that Nebii Hhudur decided to visit the house of a poor labourer in Mogadiscio. Now, this was after the Italians came to Somalia, and many men were working for them as coolies, on the roads and in the building of offices and houses. This labourer was not skilled in any craft, and he received for his work only 1½ lire a day, which was not enough to keep himself and his wife.

When Nebii Hhudur knocked at the door, the wife of the labourer answered.

"I am a stranger to this city," Nebii Hhudur said, "and I have been journeying for many days and nights, and have had nothing to eat these past forty-eight hours. Could you give me a little rice, perhaps, or a bit of jowari?"

The woman asked him to enter the house.

"We are very poor, as you can see,' 'she said, "and at the moment we have only one small dish of jowari for our food this day. But you are welcome to share it with us, if you will wait until my man comes home from work."

Nebii Hhudur agreed, and said he would spend the rest of the afternoon at the mosque, praying.

Then, when the day was over, Nebii Hhudur returned from the mosque, and shared the meal of jowari with the labourer and his wife. Afterwards, he departed, blessing them, and saying he would pray for them.

The next morning, when the labourer and his wife rose up, they thought they would have no food to begin the day. The dish of jowari had been emptied the night before, when the stranger ate with them.

But when they looked at the corner of the room where the cooking vessels and the charcoal burner stood, there was the dish of jowari, full again. Indeed, so full was it that the jowari had run over the edges and was now spilling into a pile on the floor. As they watched, it grew and grew, until the whole room was nearly filled with jowari.

Then the labourer and his wife knew that the stranger had been Nebii Hhudur.

And so, giving thanks to God, they sold the jowari and bought camels with the money, and were never poor again.

5. ABANA WYS AND THE TUB OF OIL

(NOTE : Although the Abana Wys stories are Arabic in origin, they have undoubtedly been changed a good deal through being told for many years in Somaliland. The character of Haroun Raschid appears in Burton's translations of Arabic folk-tales, and in James Elroy Flecker's "Hassan", as the Caliph of Bagdad. Here, he is described as Sultan of all Arabia. It is interesting to note that in "Hassan", Jafar is Vizier, or Minister of State, while in this story, Jafar is marked out for that post but meets an untimely death before he can achieve it. Probably Abana Wys is the "Abu Nawas" mentioned in "Hassan". The name used among Somalis, however, is definitely Abana Wys, and Wys is a fairly common name here.)

Many hundreds of years ago, there lived in the city of Jidda a man called Abana Wys. Now, Abana was a worthless sort of creature in some ways. He did as little work as possible, and his days were spent in wine-drinking and laughter. But he had the great gift of a nimble wit, and managed therefore to make his living with very little effort. Even the great Sultan loved his company, and would pay for it, because Abana Wys could make him laugh when he felt despondent.

Now the Sultan Haroun Raschid was at that time Sultan of all Arabia, and a man of enormous wealth and power. He had one daughter, of whom he was very fond, a beautiful girl with silken skin and graceful limbs and eyes soft and luminous as the dusk.

There worked in the Sultan's palace a young man named Jafar, a lad of high birth, but not wealthy. He worked as a clerk and writer of letters, and Haroun Raschid grew to admire the boy's trustworthiness and discretion.

But it happened that the young princess and Jafar fell in love with each other, and when they approached the girl's father about the matter, Haroun Raschid was exceedingly angry.

"To have my daughter marry a mere quill-scratcher?" he roared. "The daughter of Haroun Raschid, Sultan of all Arabia? Never! Better were I to become like the most miserable shoemaker or beggar of alms, rather than consent to this outrage!"

The two young people begged and pleaded, and the princess was all sweetness to her father. And Haroun Raschid saw that his daughter had a will of stone, and that her mind was made up to marry Jafar. Finally, he consented to the marriage.

"But," said he, "it will be on one condition—that you wait until you have proved yourself worthy of the post of Vizier, my young Jafar. At that time, I shall bestow upon you a rich estate, and then you may marry my daughter."

Jafar looked dismayed.

"But, oh Sultan," said the young man, "she is the most beautiful girl in all Arabia, and I am only human. Cannot we have a secret marriage now?"

"I have spoken," Haroun Raschid said. "You will not make love to my daughter, or even go near to her, until I give you permission."

The princess and Jafar were forced to agree to this condition, although it saddened their hearts. But Jafar resolved to work harder than ever, and to rise in the court as rapidly as he could.

Now, one day the Sultan was walking with Jafar in his garden, when they came upon an orange tree with one single fruit. This fruit was like a small sun, a bright and perfect globe, and it gleamed in the morning light. But unfortunately it was too high to reach.

"Here," said the Sultan, "you step on my shoulders, Jafar, and pick that orange for me, since it is too high for one man to reach."

"No," Jafar protested. "You are the Sultan of all Arabia, and I cannot step on your shoulders. I pray you, then, step on my shoulders and reach the fruit."

"No," Haroun Raschid replied. "I am an old man, and it may be that I am somewhat more stout than I was in my youth. For me to step on your shoulders, my good Jafar, could only be disastrous to us both. I command you, therefore, to step on my shoulder and reach up for that orange."

So Jafar did as Haroun Raschid ordered. And as he stood on the Sultan's shoulders, the thought came to him that here, despite his title of Sultan of all Arabia, was only a fat old man, after all. And Jafar could not put the thought from his mind.

Now it happened that Abana Wys that day was wandering past the Sultan's garden, and as Jafar stepped on Haroun Raschid's shoulders, Abana looked over the wall and saw the pair.

"Aha!" said Abana to himself. "Here is an interesting spectacle. Now I predict that we shall have some trouble before long. Young Jafar will, if I am not mistaken, go to the princess this very night. And worst of all, you, my good Abana, belong to the Birmakii, which is, alas, Jafar's tribe!"

The same day Abana Wys appeared before the Sultan.

"My lord," he began, in his most humble manner, "Excellent Sultan, Star of Arabia, I come to beg a favour."

The Sultan smiled.

"What is it this time, my friend?" he asked. "You are in debt again, no oubt, or you have no money for this evening's drinking. Your wild habits will be the ruin of you yet, Abana."

Abana Wys looked shocked.

"You mistake me, oh Sultan," he protested. "No, my request is of a serious nature, a matter of great import. As you know, I belong to the Birmakii. Now, having grown disgusted with that tribe's stupidity, I would leave them forever. Will you have a sign burned on the skin of my arm, and also write me a letter which I may carry around with me, saying that I renounce the Birmakii and am no longer of that tribe?"

The Sultan Haroun Raschid stared at Abana.

"You have made some mad requests in your time, Abana Wys," he said, "but this is the maddest I have yet heard. Do I understand that you wish to renounce your tribe, which should be like your mother and your father to you?"

Abana Wys stamped about the room and cursed at the top of his voice.

"The Birmakii!" he shouted, "may their livers harden to stone! May the clouds in the sky avoid passing over their path! May their stock die of plague, and may their camels get tick-fever! A thousand million curses on their stupidity and thievery! May I never mention the name of Birmakii again!"

The Sultan was astonished.

"You are a strange man, Abana," he said. "But if you feel so strongly about it, I will do as you ask. The skin of your arm will be burned with my seal, and I will give a letter into your hand, saying you renounce your tribe from this time forward."

"A thousand thanks, oh supreme Sultan!" cried Abana Wys, grasping Haroun Raschid's hand in gratitude.

And so it was done.

Now, for the next year, there was peace and quiet in the city of Jidda, and at the court there was harmony. Jafar continued to rise in the estimation of Haroun Raschid, and the royal household seemed happy and contented.

Then, one day, as Haroun Raschid was walking by himself in his garden, he chanced to see his daughter. And with her, to the amazement of the Sultan, there was a small child! As the princess saw her father, she fled into her own apartments, and terror showed in her eyes.

Haroun Raschid knew then that the child was indeed the son of Jafar and the princess, and that Jafar had disobeyed the Sultan's command.

The wrath of Haroun Raschid was terrible to see. He commanded that Jafar, and all of Jafar's tribe, should be beheaded.

It was a time of suffering that followed. The whole city of Jidda was in a torment, and the prison courtyard ran with blood, as the heads of all the Birmakii were cut off by the royal executioner. The wise men and the royal ministers pleaded, and the princess wept, but to no avail. One by one, the Birmakii were killed, and the handsome young Jafar was the first to go.

Then the Sultan asked if all the Birmakii had been killed.

"Every one of them," the executioner told him, "except one man—Abana Wys."

"So!" roared Haroun Raschid, completely forgetting his agreement with Abana, "he still lives! Well, he is an amusing fellow, and I used to like him, but he is Birmakii, and he must die. Bring him at once."

The executioner looked flustered.

"The only trouble, oh Sultan," he said, "is that no one can find Abana Wys. He has completely disappeared."

And so a great search was started for Abana. The Sultan's soldiers looked everywhere in the city, and beyond the city, but no trace of him could they find.

The wise men and counsellors were called in, and the magicians, and they consulted together and decided to try "faal" to find Abana. Now, to make magic by "faal", it is necessary to have a string of wooden prayer-beads, and to count these off in a strange and complex fashion known only to sorcerers. Then, the beads will fall in such a way that those who know the secrets of "faal" can read the answer.

The magic of "faal" was therefore done, and after much discussion, the magicians finally told the Sultan where Abana Wys was hiding.

"He is about five miles from the city," they said, "and he is living in a sea of oil."

The Sultan was annoyed.

"Have I wise men or have I fools?" he cried. "A sea of oil! Whoever heard of such a thing? Even the mad beggars in the streets would tell you that the sea is made of water and not oil!"

But the magicians only shook their heads sadly.

"This is all we can tell you," said they. "Abana Wys is in the country, and he is living in a sea of oil. More than that we cannot say."

So Haroun Raschid ordered the whole countryside to be searched for Abana Wys.

For days and weeks the soldiers searched for the missing Abana, and then, finally, they succeeded in finding him.

He was living about five miles from the town, in an enormous pool in the rocks, which he had filled with olive oil. In the oil he sat quite comfortably all day, protected from the heat of the sun, pondering his unique situation. When they brought him to the Sultan Haroun Raschid laughed for the first time in many months.

"So, my friend, you thought you could get away by fooling my wise men and magicians!" he cried.

"A man must look after himself," Abana replied.

"But now," the Sultan said, "unfortunately, we shall have to kill you."

"I was afraid you would forget your promise," Abana Wys said, "so I did not want to be found until you had become more calm, when I could show you this letter without arousing your anger."

And he pulled out the letter the Sultan had given him, and showed the mark on his arm which signified that Abana Wys had rejected the Birmakii tribe.

Haroun Raschid laughed and laughed.

"Very well, Abana," he said finally. "You shall not die. But tell me one thing—how did you know it would be useful to reject the Birmakii?"

But Abana Wys only smiled.

6.   ABANA WYS AND THE BED-BUGS

Now it is well known that in the city of Jidda, many years ago, some men were the slaves of wine, and lived not by the Prophet's teaching. And it is further known that Abana Wys, that sharp-witted man, learned though he was in the ways of cleverness and talented in the ways of laughter, had very few scruples against drinking. Indeed, most of his evenings were spent in the wine-shops of the town, drinking and story-spinning with his friends. Then, after midnight, when the poems he recited no longer made any sense, Abana Wys would stagger back through the almost deserted streets to his little house, where he would fall snoring on the bed.

The house of Abana Wys was a miserable place, small and cramped, with an earth floor and one tiny slit of a window. It was none too clean, either, and the bed of Abana Wys abounded in bed-bugs.

But every evening, so drunk was Abana Wys that he fell asleep at once and did not notice the bed-bugs at all, although they bit him continually. In the morning he would arise, very sore and angry, and tell everyone in the street that some rogue had hit him the evening before, or that he had fallen into a thorn-bush, and as proof he would point to the red welts on his skin.

One day, while Abana Wys was in the town, the Sultan Haroun Raschid visited his house.

Seeing the bed crawling with the ugly little insects, the Sultan was amazed.

"How is it," he asked Abana's servant, "that your master can sleep nights, with these little beasts crawling all over him and biting him in his tenderest parts?"

"It is easily explained," the lad replied. "Abana Wys —may God forgive him—is always drunk when he comes home, and so does not notice these pests."

The Sultan was horrified.

"We shall see," he said, "how Abana feels about it when the wine is not upon him."

And so that evening the Sultan sought out Abana Wys in the city, and he found him before Abana had gone to the wine-shops.

"Tonight," Haroun Raschid said, "you will come with me, and stay in my palace for the evening, and no wine will be drunk."

And so it was done. And when the Sultan accompanied Abana Wys to the little hovel, no wine had passed the lips of either man.

When Abana looked inside his house, and saw the insects creeping over his bed, he shouted in alarm.

"Someone has brought these horrible creatures to my house! One of my enemies is plotting against me!"

"No," Haroun Raschid said, "these bed-bugs are there every night. Most evenings you are too drunk to notice them. Tonight you shall sleep here, among these pests, and tomorrow we shall see if you are not a better man. Perhaps a night here without the benefit of wine will teach you the folly of letting your house go untended and uncared for, while you spout verse in the wine-shops! No more shall you drink, Abana, for by the Prophet's beard, if you do, one of these days you will die of poison from these insects, and who then would amuse me in my hours of sadness?"

Abana Wys, therefore, settled himself down for the night among his bugs. But there was no sleep for him. When he had brushed a bed-bug from his neck, another bit him on the foot. And when he had attended to that, yet another was biting the small of his back, or a shoulder where he could not reach. The night was torment and agony for Abana Wys.

The next morning he arose, tired and disgusted. But instead of swearing to look after his house better, Abana sat down and wrote a letter to the Sultan Haroun Raschid.

"Honoured and Most Mighty Sultan," the letter ran, "Jewel of Jidda, Slayer of the Infidel, Protector of all Arabia, and Wonder of the East, I would say only a few words concerning the question of bed-bugs, a matter which itches both in my mind and over my entire body. Although I slept but little last night, yet am I not embittered, for a philosopher views all things in the light of eternity. I would not have innocent creatures die in order to ensure the sound sleep of one so humble as myself, when that sleep can be obtained by simpler measures. Oh great Sultan, I beg you to give me leave to drink again, and both myself and my insects can live in peace, neither bothering the other."

When Haroun Raschid received the letter, he was so amused that he agreed to let Abana Wys drink wine as before. Abana, much relieved, sent his small servant boy out to buy two bottles of wine, giving him the last coin he had in his purse.

However,~the boy was in such a hurry to get back that he slipped and fell at the doorway of Abana's house. The bottles of wine crashed to the ground and broke, and the wine ran over the floor of the house.

"Now," said Abana, "that is just the sort of thing that would happen to me. Fool, you have given the earth the drink!"

But Abana was ever a philosophical man.

"Who knows," he added gravely, "perhaps the earth, too, craved protection against the bugs, and who am I to deny it ?"

And so it will be seen that Abana Wys, although not as sensible as other men, had the kindest heart in all Jidda.

7. THE BEARD OF ABANA WYS

It happened that Abana Wys, when he was getting on in years, grew an enormous beard. Such a fine beard had never been seen in Jidda, and the people would turn in the street and point at Abana Wys, saying that although the man himself was fat and ugly, he gained a certain distinction from the richness and luxuriant growth of his beard.

Abana Wys, having as usual squandered any money that came his way, approached the Sultan one day in the hope of raising a little cash by his swift words.

"Oh Sultan," he said, "have I not made you laugh, many a time, when the affairs of state weighed heavy on your mind?"

"It is true," Haroun Raschid answered, smiling.

"And have you not wondered, many a time, at the speed of my jests and the quickness of my wit?"

"It is true," the Sultan replied again.

"Then, oh Master of all Arabia," said Abana Wys hope-fully, "could you, perhaps, on the strength of this old friendship of ours, lend me a small amount of money?" The Sultan Haroun Raschid laughed.

"What?" he cried. "Have I become a money-lender? No, Abana, I will not lend money to you, but I will give you a good sum."

Abana Wys fell down at the Sultan's feet in surprise and gratitude.

"May the everlasting blessings of Allah be upon your name!" he gasped. "May your sons rule the earth! May . ."

"Wait," said Haroun Raschid, "there is one condition."

Abana looked up at him suspiciously.

"You must sell me your beard," the Sultan said.

Then Abana Wys was in a quandary. He could not bear the thought of parting with his beautiful beard, which had taken so long to grow, but on the other hand, he needed the money badly. At last he agreed.

"Bring your barbers," he said bravely. "You may have it."

Haroun Raschid laughed again.

"No," he said, "you may keep it for the time being, and I shall claim it when I see fit."

The next day was a festival, and the notable men of the city went to the Sultan's palace for a feast. Although Abana Wys was of humble birth, he was always invited to the Sultan's great feasts, and he appeared with his beard splendidly combed and shining.

The dinner that day was exceptionally fine, with all manner of rich food, and the attendance was large. The Sultan planned to have Abana Wys' beard cut off after the meal to amuse the company.

Abana's tastes were simple, but he never lost an opportunity to do justice to the Sultan's food. On this day, he stuffed himself until his belly swelled. Then, settling down on his cushion, he pushed his platter away from him, and opened his mouth as though to yawn. And from his throat such a sound of repletion arose, that it might have been the thunder before a storm, or the roar of a lion in the desert night.

The Sultan pretended to be amazed.

"How is it," he asked, "that you can make such a loud sound? A gentle sound of satisfaction is only proper, but could you not, for the sake of delicacy, cloak this mighty outburst in your thick beard?"

Abana Wys glanced at him with twinkling eyes.

"Forgive me, powerful Sultan," he answered, "if I correct you. But you forget—I have no beard. This one belongs to you!"

8.   ABANA WYS AND THE TWO CORPSES

Abana Wys, as it is well known, married a wife rather late in his life. The woman could not be described as the most beautiful of women, but she, like Abana, had a talent for making money by her wits. And so the pair got along very well.

One morning Abana Wys sought an audience with the Sultan Haroun Raschid, ruler of all Arabia. The Sultan agreed to see him, and when Abana came into his presence, he was astonished at the sad appearance of the rotund little man. Abana was weeping bitterly, and his beard was slightly ragged where he had torn it in his distress.

"By all the Djinn!" Haroun Raschid exclaimed, "why do you look so glum, Abana, you who are always so gay?"

"Ah, Sultan," Abana said woefully, "I must tell you that my wife died this morning."

"I am sorry indeed to hear it," the Sultan said sympathetically. "Was she ill for long?"

"No," Abana said. "It was a sudden sickness that had killed the poor creature before I realized how seriously ill she was. Ah, it is a hard life! And now, wretched man that I am, I have not even enough money to give her a decent burial."

The Sultan touched Abana gently on the shoulder.

"Do not worry, my friend," he said, "I will give you the money. I have always enjoyed your company, and it would be a poor thing indeed if Haroun Raschid could not give a much-needed sum to such a good companion."

"A thousand thanks," Abana said gratefully, "and may Allah cause you to prosper for a hundred years more, and may you sire four dozen sons!"

And he went away.

As it happened, however, that same morning the wife of Abana Wys went to the wife of the Sultan, looking very sad and dejected.

"What is the matter, my good woman?" the Sultana asked. "You look very sorrowful this morning."

"Indeed, madan," the wife of Abana said, "I am very sorrowful. Poor Abana Wys has just died."

The Sultan's wife looked sympathetic.

"I am sorry to hear it," she said. "He was a gay, amusing man. You must feel badly indeed."

"I do," the other answered, "for I loved Abana dearly, despite his peculiarities. The worst part of it is that I can't even give him a decent burial, as he has left me without a thing in the world."

"Well, well," the Sultan's wife said, "we shall soon fix that. I can let you have the money, and I am sure my husband the Sultan would agree that I was right in giving it to you."

"A thousand thanks!" cried Abana's wife. "And may you be everlastingly blessed with happiness!"

And so she went away.

But that evening, the Sultan Haroun Raschid spoke to his wife about the matter

"I was sad to hear that Abana Wys' wife died this morning," he said.

The Sultana stared at him.

"Oh, no, you are mistaken," she said. "It was Abana Wys himself who died!"

The Sultan frowned at her.

"Did I not myself see Abana this morning, and give him money for his wife's funeral? Do not talk nonsense to me!"

"And did I not see Abana's wife," the lady said, "and give her money for Abana's funeral? Indeed, my lord, I swear it on the Kitab!"

Then they looked at each other.

"This Abana is a clever man," the Sultan said grimly, "but we shall see. Come, we will go to his house this minute.

Haroun Raschid and his wife went to Abana's house, therefore, and knocked at the door. However, Abana had heard them approaching, and when the Sultan and his wife entered the little house, they saw two corpses lying on the bed, stretched out, it seemed, in the stiff coldness of death.

"Alas!" the Sultan cried, "I have just injured your name, my good Abana! I have doubted your word! A thousand pardons! See—they are both dead!"

The Sultan's wife wept a little.

"Yes, they are both dead," she said. "And two fine people they were."

"It is merciful that they both died on the same day," the Sultan mused. "Why, Abana must have died soon after his wife this morning."

"No, indeed," his wife corrected him, "Abana died first, since I saw his wife this morning. She must have come back home with the funeral money and died soon after."

"Woman!" the Sultan roared furiously, "do not presume to correct me! I tell you Abana's wife died first!"

"And I tell you that Abana died first!"

"Abana's wife, idiot and devil-begotten!"

"Abana, stubborn mule!"

At this moment, the kind-hearted Abana, who could not bear to see people quarrelling, and who was also a little concerned about his own reputation, sat up abruptly on the bed.

"Sultan," he cried, "you are quite right, obviously! My wife died first!"

Immediately, Abana's wife sat up, her eyes flashing with rage.

"Dolt!" she screamed at him, "you died first! How dare you say otherwise?"

The Sultan and his wife stared in astonishment at the couple. Then Haroun Raschid laughed until he was weak.

"Ah, Abana," he cried, "you have won again! Keep the funeral money, and may you both live to be a hundred!"

9. ABANA WYS AND THE BLIND THIEF

One day when the Sultan Haroun Raschid was feeling depressed, he called Abana Wys to him.

"Abana," he said, "I am sad today. Can you make me laugh?"

"Of course," said Abana confidently, "nothing is easier."

So they took a small donkey-cart and drove outside the city of Jidda. Soon they saw a blind man, hobbling along the road with a stick to guide him.

"Sultan," Abana Wys said, "I beg you to lend me that gold bracelet you wear."

And so Haroun Raschid gave the gold bracelet to Abana.

"Sit here," said Abana, "and be very quiet. We shall see what happens."

Then Abana picked up a stick and hobbled along the road to meet the blind man.. As he approached, he bumped into the old fellow and jostled him off his path.

"Here, you clumsy dog!" the blind man shouted angrily. "Can't you watch where you're going?"

"I'm sorry," Abana whined. "But I am sightless. Alas I have no eyes."

"Ah, friend," the other sighed, "I, too, am blind. It is a hard life."

"Hard indeed," said Abana, "with few enough people to take pity on me. But it has its rewards, just the same. Feel this bracelet—it is of the purest gold. The good Sultan Haroun Raschid gave it to me this morning."

The blind man took the bracelet in his hands.

"It is indeed pure gold," he murmured, touching the metal with expert fingers. "You are a fortunate man."

He fondled the bracelet for a moment, and then, without warning, he darted away and began to run down the road, the bracelet in his hand.

The blind man ran very swiftly, but since it was a rough road, he stumbled from time to time, and Abana was able to get quite close to him. Then Abana picked up a small stone.

"May God give this stone eyes," he shouted, "to make up for my blindness, and may the stone find the back of that thief's neck!"

And he threw the stone, aiming very carefully. The stone hit the blind thief on the back of the neck, and the man yelled, both in pain and fear.

"Wallahi!" he cried. "A stone with eyes! Whoever heard of a stone with eyes! Here, take your bracelet, for you have a djinn working for you!"

With that there was a loud sound, like unto a wild roaring wind or a crash of thunder. It was the Sultan Haroun Raschid laughing.

"You have done well," he cried. "And now the blind man may keep that bracelet, and here is another the same for you, my good Abana!"

B. SOMALI TALES

1. THE GREAT SURPRISE

One day two thieves chanced to be walking along a road near some jowari fields. Looking across the fields, they saw a man ploughing. The animals which pulled the plough were two fine oxen. The thieves looked at one another.

"I have never seen such fine fat oxen," the first man said.

"Truly, they are wonderful beasts," the other mused.

"We could get a large price for those oxen in the 'magala'," the first thief went on.

The other nodded.

"In truth, we could get a great deal of money for them," he agreed. "But how could we take them away? A man who is ploughing is not going to leave his oxen, and I notice he wears a long knife at his belt."

The first thief smiled.

"Ah, my friend, what it is to have brains!" he cried. "Listen to my idea. You will go on that side of the field, and I will stay here on this side. Then I will begin howling and shouting, and soon the ploughman will come over to find out what is the matter. Then, after two hours, I will reveal the reason to him. By that time, you will have got far away with the first of the oxen. I will undertake to look after the other. We will meet at that place some distance from here, where we had our fire last evening."

The second thief laughed scornfully.

"How can you keep the ploughman standing there for two hours?" he asked. "And how can your get away with the other of the oxen? This is foolishness!"

"Trust me," said the first, "and I promise you will not be disappointed."

And so it came about that the second thief stole quietly around to the far side of the jowari field, while the first thief stayed by the side of the road.

And after the second thief had hidden himself among the bushes, the first thief began shouting in a loud voice.

"By God!" he shouted, "this is most strange! Amazing! Wonderful!"

The ploughman looked up from his work, and then bent again to the plough.

"Incredible!" went on the thief, his voice growing louder with each exclamation, "who would have thought it possible? What a wondrous thing! What a surprise!"

The ploughman looked up again, and the thief, encouraged, roared and bellowed more than ever.

Finally the ploughman could stand the suspense no longer. He left his plough and his oxen and walked over to the place where the thief sat.

"What is this, my friend?" the ploughman asked, "I hear you screaming 'Most wonderful!' I beg you to tell me what the mystery is."

But the thief went on shouting, and ignored the earnest ploughman.

"Is it not the greatest wonder of the earth?" he howled. "Most strange and queer it is! Amazing! Incredible!"

The ploughman again begged him to impart the secret.

"What is this thing that causes so much wonder in you, friend?" he asked.

But the thief merely went on yelling.

"Wonderful! Amazing! Incredible!"

The curiosity of the ploughman was now thoroughly aroused, and he pleaded with the thief to tell him what great surprise was causing him so much amazement. But the thief ignored him entirely and kept on roaring after the same manner.

For two hours the thief shouted, and for two hours the honest ploughman, all agog with curiosity, begged him to tell his secret.

Finally the ploughman became impatient.

"Traveller," he said angrily, "are you mad, or what? Surely you must be mad to bellow in this fashion for all this time and still refuse to tell me what is so wondrous strange. Either you will tell me this instant, or I will give you a crack over the skull with my knife-handle, a crack that you won't forget for many a long day."

Then the thief fell silent. After a few minutes he gazed up at the ploughman, and smiled in a friendly way.

"Why, good ploughman," the thief explained, "I shall tell you straightaway what has surprised me. It is nothing other than the sight of a man ploughing with one ox, and that one wearing a double yoke. How is it possible? Is your ox a devil or a magic beast, that it can plough in this fashion?"

Then the ploughman's anger burst forth.

"What nonsense have I wasted my time on!" he cried. "Of course I plough with two oxen, just like every other man! You are indeed mad!"

"Oh no," said the thief, "one ox is all you have. Look and see if I am not right."

The ploughman glanced around, and sure enough, one ox only stood in the field, and the other half of the yoke was empty.

"How is this?", the ploughman cried. "I had two oxen when I came across here to ask you why you roared and yelled in this way!"

"Ah, no, my friend," the thief insisted, "I have been here all day, and you have had only one ox."

Then the good ploughman grew alarmed.

"Some devil has been at work here!" he said in a loud voice. "Some djinn has spirited off my ox! But I am a strong man—be he devil or djinn or human being, he will not get away with this theft! I shall track him down, and kill him, and get my ox back! Just you wait and see!"

And the sturdy ploughman set off at a run. As he drew near the plough and the remaining ox, he sighted the tracks that the other thief and the ox had made in their flight, and off he ran, following the tracks into the bush.

As soon as the ploughman was out of sight, the first thief rose, and quietly led away the ox that was left.

When the ploughman returned, dusty and tired, after losing the tracks in the grass and bushes, he found his second ox gone also.

And as for the thieves, they ate well that night.

2. TALE OF TWO THIEVES

Two thieves chanced to see a man walking along a road one day, leading a good fat ram and carrying a large vessel of ghee.

"See that traveller yonder?" one whispered to the other. "How can we cheat him?"

The other thief smiled knowingly.

"I have a plan," he replied.

And so it happened that the thieves waited by the roadside, and one of them hid himself in some bushes. The other began shouting and moaning in an anguished voice.

"Oh ye Muslims!" he cried. "will ye desert your own?"

The traveller was a good-hearted man, and so he stopped by the thief and spoke in a kindly way to him.

"Why are you so troubled, friend?"

"I am a blind man," the thief replied, "and there is no one to lead me to the town. Alas, a man without eyes might better be dead!"

"I will lead you," the traveller said, "and you shall lead my ram, for I cannot lead both you and the ram at the same time and carry this heavy vessel as well. Here, I will put the ram's rope into your hand."

And so they set out. But after they had gone a few miles, the thief began to cry out again.

"Alas!" he groaned, "I feel that the rope in my hands is lighter, and I fear the ram has slipped the lead and escaped into the bushes! I am a poor unfortunate blind man, who brings trouble upon those who would help me! Woe unto me!"

The traveller was worried about the loss of his ram, but he was a good man, and had pity in his heart, and so he did not get angry with the other man.

"Never mind," he said, "I had better go and look for the ram, but you can stay and look after this vessel of ghee while I am away. In that way you will be of assistance to me after all."

The thief agreed gladly, with many protestations of goodwill and eagerness to help.

And so the traveller set off to look for the ram, and the thief remained with the vessel of ghee.

The unfortunate traveller returned after some hours, empty-handed. But alas, neither the blind man nor the vessel of ghee was anywhere to be seen.

3. THE MAN WHO SWORE FALSELY

(NOTE : This story is supposed to be a true one. Swearing falsely on the Qoran has, if anything, even greater association of wrongdoing and sin than, for us, swearing falsely on the Bible.)

One time, not so long ago, there lived a man whose tribal group was camped between Odweina and Gudubi. It happened that he killed a man from another tribe, although the man had done him no harm and had not looted his camels or stolen one of his daughters. After he killed the man, the murderer hid the body in the bushes. So well did he hide it, that no one could find the body or prove the murderer's guilt.

But the dead man's tribe suspected the murderer, and so they went to his tribe to make enquiries.

"Is the man whom we suspect living here?" they asked.

"Yes," the tribal elders replied. "But we cannot hand him over to you. He denies having murdered your tribesman, and we do not know whether he is guilty or not. And, indeed, if no one can find the body, it may be that your tribesman was taken by a lion. Under the circumstances, we cannot fix a compensation for the man's death."

"We do not want a compensation in camels," the dead man's tribe said. "This only do we ask—that that man, your tribesman, since he denies having murdered, should swear by Allah's Name on the Kitab, one hundred times, his innocence."

Then the murderer's tribe went to him, and they were greatly afraid.

"If you did this thing," they said, "admit it, and we will pay compensation gladly. But do not swear by God's Name to a lie."

But the murderer was afraid in his heart, and would not own to the killing.

And so he swore on the Qoran, saying "Wa Allah", "Wa Allah", "Wa Allah". And he finished swearing his innocence for the ninety-ninth time, on God's Name. Then, as he put his hand again on the Holy Book to swear a lie by God's Name for the hundredth time, he grew pale, and the life went from him, and he died.

4. THE FOUR WISE COUNSELLORS

Once there was a great and powerful Sultan, who had a beautiful daughter of marriageable age. It came to pass that a certain man arrived one day to ask the Sultan for his daughter's hand in marriage. This man was wealthy, and had many thousands of camels, and was highly respected in the country, and so the Sultan agreed to the request.

"Very well, marry her," he said, "and the two of you shall live within my royal dwelling, for I could not be parted from my daughter."

And so it was arranged.

As it happened, on the same day another young man came to the Sultan and asked for the princess's hand in marriage. This man was even wealthier than the first, and had tens of thousands of camels, and was very highly respected in the country. And so the Sultan agreed to the request.

"Very well," said he, "you shall marry her, and the two of you will live within my royal dwelling, for I could not be parted from my daughter."

However, the great Sultan told neither young man about the other. To the first young man he said :

"You must see your wife only in the daytime. If you ever see her at night, you will be killed at once. It is my command."

And to the second young man he said :

"You must see your wife only at night. If ever you look upon her in the daytime, you will be put to death at once. It is my command."

And so it was arranged.

The marriages took place, and the two young men became members of the Sultan's council, and everything went very well indeed. The first husband saw his wife in the daytime, and the second husband saw his wife at night. Everyone was exceedingly happy, especially when the Sultan's daughter gave birth to a fine son.

Years passed, and the baby grew into a sturdy little boy of which any father might be proud.

One day, there was a meeting of the Sultan's counsellors. They were all gathered in the council chamber, and among them were the two husbands of the Sultan's daughter. As it happened, the Sultan's young grandson was playing in the corridor outside the council chamber. In the middle of the meeting, the boy chanced to open the door and peep inside.

"Ah! Here is my son!" cried the first husband.

"There you are, my boy—come to your father!" exclaimed the second husband, at precisely the same moment.

There was a terrible silence in the council room. The two husbands glared at each other.

"What? Do you insult me thus?" cried the first husband.

"This is a strange and dishonourable joke you play on me!" raged the second husband.

All the counsellors of the Sultan held their breath. Even the mighty Sultan did not feel quite at ease in the situation.

Joke?" roared the first husband. "Is it a joke to call my own son my son?"

Your son?" shouted the second husband. "What impudence is this, that you call yourself the father of my boy?"

The Sultan sighed a ponderous sigh. It was obvious to him that the story must now be told.

When it was explained to the two husbands, they were more angry than ever. Both wanted the boy, whose paternal parentage, indeed, was far from being clearly established. And both wanted to keep the Sultan's lovely daughter as his wife.

Many were the arguments, threats, shouts and exhortations that resounded through the royal dwelling. At length, the Sultan himself decided to call in the wisest elders in the land, and those fully versed in the Laws, in order that they might give their advice and in some manner settle the dispute.

The elders were accordingly consulted. These venerable greybeards arrived carrying massive texts in which the entire Laws and commentaries on the Laws were set down. For many days the elders discussed together, quoting this law and that, with many a finely turned phrase and many a subtle sentence. But, alas, no agreement could be reached. In all the weighty volumes, no such case was recorded. These books, rich in the wisdom of the ages, were thumbed through again and again, and the elders talked and argued and considered and summarized until their voices were hoarse and their brains were in a whirl. But to no avail. The first husband wanted both the boy and the Sultan's charming daughter, and the second husband wanted precisely the same.

Finally, in desperation, the Sultan sent the elders away.

"All our wisest elders have failed to come to a judgment," said he. "Therefore now we shall have another council. When wisdom fails, folly may be wise. Four hashish addicts will be our counsellors."

The Sultan's counsellors and the first husband and the second husband and the Sultan's delightful daughter all held up their hands in horror. But the great Sultan was adamant.

Four hashish addicts were finally collected and brought to the Sultan's palace. They entered the royal dwelling slowly, but with a certain dreamy grace, and from time to time they halted to pirouette gravely, smiling their sad gay faraway smiles.

The Sultan explained to them that the situation was somewhat difficult and embarrassing.

"My daughter," said he, "is married to two men, both worthy persons and highly respected in the country. The first is her husband in the daytime, and the second is her husband at night. She has, unfortunately, only one son. Now, each husband has discovered the existence of the other, and both are quite upset. Both desire to keep the son and my daughter (whose charms are admittedly considerable). How we resolve the problem is up to you."

The hashish addicts put on expressions of the greatest mock-seriousness, each placing one finger on his forehead, as if in deep thought. They whispered together for a moment, and then glanced up, smiling calmly.

"There is no problem here," their spokesman said. "All we need to do is to call in the boy and ask him which of these two men is his father."

And so the small grandson of the Sultan was accordingly called in.

"Which of these two men is your father, little one?" one of the hashish addicts asked kindly.

The boy was trembling with fright at the sight of the dignified counsellors, the two fierce-looking husbands, the smiling hashish addicts, and the grand Sultan. Finally he spoke.

"There," he said, in a weak little voice, "that's my father."

And he pointed towards the first husband.

"This is insufferable!" cried the second husband, "The boy is confused! We must test again!"

The hashish addicts only smiled.

"Very well," said they. "The other shall go into the corridor and you shall remain in the room. We shall see what happens then."

And so it was agreed. The first husband departed from the council room, and the second husband remained.

Again the small boy was asked to point out his father.

The grandson of the Sultan looked around carefully, and finally he spoke.

"He's not here," he announced firmly.

A great shout arose from the throats of the Sultan's counsellors and the first husband and the second husband and the Sultan's daughter and the powerful Sultan himself.

"How is it that the boy has thus chosen between them?" the Sultan asked.

"It is very simple," the hashish addicts replied modestly. "The boy has chosen the man who appeared in the daytime. The other, quite naturally, he has never seen, since he was asleep at nights when the second husband appeared. The first husband, therefore, will take the boy as his son. The second husband will, in a like manner of justice, take the Sultan's comely daughter as his wife. In our opinion, there has been a great amount of fuss over nothing."

And so it was agreed.

5. THE GHEE AND THE MILK

There once was a man whose wife was very fond of
ghee. When they ate their evening meal together, the
wife would always put the small pool of ghee on her side
of the ricebowl, so that she might mix it with her rice.
The milk she would place in the ricebowl at her husband's
side. This procedure went on for months and years, the
man always eating the milk with his rice, and the woman
the ghee.

Finally, however, the patience of the man was exhausted. He had told her time after time that he would like
some ghee on his rice, but never once had he got it. So
he decided to do the cooking himself one day. He cooked
the evening meal, and placed the ghee on his side of the
bowl and milk on hers. When the wife sat down to eat,
she looked up at him and smiled her most kindly smile.

Then she took up her spoon.

"When I think of the words you said to me yesterday,
my beloved husband," she murmured, "it rives my heart—
like this!"

And she drew a line through the rice from her side to
his, so that the ghee flowed in a little channel onto her
portion of the meal.

The husband also smiled, and took up his spoon.

"And when I remember your reply, my cherished wife,"
he replied, "it stirs my heart—like this!"

6. MIDGAN STORIES

(NOTE : These are Somali jokes. There are a great
number of jokes in Somali about the Midgan people, an
outcast tribe who do menial jobs such as sweeping, and
who are traditionally the hunters and leather-workers of
the country. The Migdan, nowadays at any rate, is very
often a clever businessman and a hard worker. He has
always been more skilled in crafts than the average Somali.

And yet, despite this, the Somalis look down on the Migdans as inferior people, and like to laugh at the Midgans' supposed stupidity.)

One evening a Midgan family journeyed out to a well to fill their water vessels. With them they carried a small baby. When the water vessels were filled, they discovered that they could not possibly carry the baby and the heavy jars at the same time. So they decided to leave the child and come back afterwards for him. But where, in all that unvarying bush country, could they leave him in a place sufficiently well-marked for them to find it again? Finally they thought of a wonderful idea, and went off happily, having left the baby right underneath the moon!

* * *

The wife of a Midgan once had a miscarriage. The Midgan was very angry. When people asked him why he was so angry, he cried.

"There! That will teach me not to pour anything into a vessel that's upside down!"

* * *

Once a Midgan got a letter from an elder of the town where his mother lived. His mother, the letter said, was ill and might even be dying. The Midgan, very upset, got a letter-writer to reply to his mother.

"Dear mother," the Midgan's letter said, "I am sorry to hear that you are sick. If you are still alive, please let me know. If however, you are dead by now, please write at once and tell me where you have hidden your money."

* * *

Once a Midgan was extremely sick. His friends came to visit him and found him lying on his bed, groaning and sweating. He was gasping for air, and was obviously in great pain. His friends asked him how he was feeling. The only answer was an increased groaning.

"You must have a terrible sickness," his friends sympathized.

The Midgan looked at them askance.

'It's not the sickness I mind," he said. "The sickness is all right. It's this pain I can't stand!"

7. WIIL WAAL AND THE SHEEP'S GULLET

(NOTE : Sultan Wiil Waal is supposed to have lived in the 16th century, and was the national hero who drove the last of the Galla kings from Jigjigga. The whole area around Jigjigga and Harar was his province. He composed many giiraar, including "The Bond Between Kings", if this is really his. What he actually did in his lifetime has probably become coloured by time to a large extent, and he himself is something of a legendary figure. Many tales are told about him, and of course their truth cannot be vouched for, as there is no common written language in Somaliland and the stories have undoubtedly changed throughout the years.

Wiil Waal was actually a Gerad, although he is generally called Sultan nowadays. But he lived before the Arabic title was commonly used here. Gerad was second in the importance-of-leaders hierarchy—(a) Baqr, (b) Gerad, (c) Ugas. A king's title depended upon how much territory he could defend and how great his wealth was. The Somali titles of Gerad and Ugas still exist here, but the less specific title of Sultan is usually used these days. I am told that in the past there were no hereditary titles here.)

Many years ago, in the country around Jigjigga, there ruled a powerful and wise Sultan by the name of Wiil Waal. He was king over the Bartire, a tribe of Darod, great in strength and wealthy with many thousands of camels.

One day it happened that Wiil Waal called all the men of the Bartire together, and told them there would be a 'shiir' or tribal meeting, on the following day.

"All the men of the Bartire must attend this meeting," the Sultan said, "for I have solemn words to impart to you. But take heed, ye tribesmen! Each man must return home now and kill the best sheep of his flock. And tomorrow, each man must bring with him a part of the sheep. But, look you, I do not say which part you must bring. That you must decide for yourselves. I say only that each must bring to the meeting that part of the animal which makes men either brothers or enemies. Go, ye Bartire, and consider well."

So the men departed from that place. And each pondered the Sultan's words, and could find no meaning in them. For what part of the animal could make men either brothers or enemies?

All day long, the Bartire elders puzzled over the words, and discussed together. But, finding no answer to the strange demand of Sultan Wiil Waal, each decided to take a chance. The sheep were slaughtered in each home that night, and the special piece of mutton was selected. One man decided to take a leg of meat to the 'shiir'. Another thought that a good saddle of mutton might please the Sultan. Another, the shoulders of the sheep. And so it went.

One man of the Bartire was very poor. In his flock, he had no more than half a dozen sheep. But, obeying his Sultan's command, he killed a fine sheep that night, and gave it to his daughter to cut up the meat.

Now this girl was about fifteen years old, and very beautiful. But as well as beauty, she also had a brain.

"Father!" she cried in alarm, "why have you killed the fattest sheep of all our tiny flock? Most certainly this is wasteful!"

"Alas," the man answered, "the Sultan Wiil Waal has demanded that each man kill his finest sheep tonight. There, now that you have finished cutting the meat, I will select this leg—it is surely as plump and tender a piece of mutton as any man is likely to bring."

"Where will you take the leg, father?" the girl asked. "We are poor, and cannot afford to give away meat."

"Alas," her father replied, "I have no choice. Sultan Wiil Waal has instructed the men of the Bartire to attend a meeting tomorrow. Each man is to bring that part of the animal which makes men either brothers or enemies. I

:an see no sense in his words, but I daresay this leg of
ny fine fat sheep will do as well as any."

Then the girl considered for a moment.

"No, father," she said finally, "you are wrong. Do not
ake the leg of mutton."

"I must," her father said, growing impatient. "Do not
:alk nonsense to me."

"But father," the girl said, "you must listen. Don't
take good meat to the council tomorrow. Take, I beg of
you, the sheep's gullet."

"What!" roared the old man. "The gullet? Could I so
insult the Sultan as to bring a sheep's gullet instead of
meat? You are mad, girl!"

"No, father," the girl insisted. "You don't understand,
and I dare not explain to you, for the Sultan himself will
explain tomorrow. But trust me and take the sheep's
gullet. If I am wrong, I will suffer the punishment in your
stead."

Then the old man thought for a long while. True, he
was very poor, and could not afford to give away meat.
Should he, then, follow his daughter's advice?

"Very well," he said at last, "you are a clever girl, and
so I will trust you and take the sheep's gullet. But what
will happen, God alone knows."

The next day, the poor man took the gullet of the
sheep and wrapped it in his robe to protect it from the
sand and dust. Then he set out for the council meeting.

There he found all the men of the Bartire, each con-
cealing a part of a sheep under his robe, and each wondering what part the others had brought.

Finally Wiil Waal himself arrived, and called for the
pieces of sheep to be brought forth. One man brought out
a leg of mutton, another a shoulder, another the liver.
another the ribs. And so it went.

When all the others had given their piece of meat to
the Sultan, the poor man stepped forward, ashamed and
anxiou?

"And what have you brought?" Wiil Waal asked.

The poor man hesitated, and finally drew the sheep's gullet out from his robe.

A great gasp went up from the men of the tribe, and then they began to shout.

"What is this? A sheep's gullet? What an insult, to offer a sheep's gullet to a Sultan!"

The poor man trembled and grew exceedingly afraid. He was too terrified to look at Wiil Waal. Then he gathered his courage and shot a glance at the Sultan's face. To his amazement, he saw that the mighty Sultan was laughing.

"Well, my friend," Wiil Waal said, "I see we have one wise man, and one only, in the tribe!"

The old man stared at him, amazed.

"Aha!" cried the Sultan, "then you did not think of this idea by yourself? Who told you to bring the gullet?"

The old man looked down at the ground, and mumbled his reply.

"My daughter," he said.

Then Sultan Wiil Waal stood up and beckoned to all the men of the tribe.

"Listen, oh ye men of the Bartire!" he said. "There is in this tribe not one wise man among you! A mere girl has made fools of you all! Hark, and I will tell you why. I did not ask you to bring meat. I asked you to bring that part of the animal which makes men either brothers or enemies. This is the symbol, and this is the wisdom I have to impart to you. The gullet receives the food. It alone makes men brothers, and it alone makes men enemies. Why do men fight? Because one man possesses much wealth while another possesses none. And because the rich man will not give freely to the poor wretch who hungers, and the anger of the hungry man is turned against the man who is fat and prosperous! And when do men become as brothers? When they help each other in time of need. When the rich are generous, and the poor hunger not. Wherefore I tell you, of ye Bartire, the gullet, the receiver of food, makes men either brothers or enemies. Mark ye, and learn."

Then the great Wiil Waal turned to the poor man.

"Your daughter, friend," he said, "is more wise than all the tribe. I will marry her, and she will be my most trusted and beloved wife!"

8. WIIL WAAL AND THE SILVER RING

It happened that two months after Sultan Wiil Waal married the clever daughter of the poor shepherd, some trouble arose among the sections of the Bartire tribe. The people concerned sent word to the Sultan, that he might come and make peace among them.

Now, Wiil Waal had two horses that he prized above all his others. One was a big black stallion and the other a fine white mare. He gave orders for his stallion to be saddled, ready for going on a journey, and then he went to his wife.

"I must go on a long journey," he said to her, "and I may be away for many months. My horse is being saddled now, and I shall leave within the hour. My white mare I shall leave here with you. But there is one thing I must demand."

"Very well," his wife said, "and what do you demand?"

Wiil Waal smiled.

"I will tell you," he said, "I know that you are in your last days of monthly sickness, and are therefore not pregnant. The white mare, also, has not conceived as yet. This day, myself and my black stallion, we are both departing on a long journey, and I have told you we may not be back for many months. When, however, we arrive back here, I want to see you with a child and the white mare with a colt. If my wish is not carried out, you will die, and the mare also. Do you understand?"

The Sultan's lovely young wife turned away.

"Nothing, oh king, could be more clear," she said, and her heart was fluttering with terror.

"Farewell, then, my beautiful wife," Wiil Waal said, "and the blessings and the peace of God be upon thy head."

It was barely two hours after daybreak when the Sultan set off, riding his black horse, along the road that led from Jigjigga to the far province that was his destination.

The Sultan's wife went out into the courtyard of the palace, and stood looking at the white mare. The mare, all unknowing of the Sultan's command, flicked her tail to brush away the flies, and neighed softly as the syce came up with a bucket of water for her to drink.

"Alas, good little mare," the Sultan's wife whispered, "What shall we do? If we do not bear offspring, my lord will have us killed. But if thou are unfaithful to thy mate, and I to mine, he will have us killed in any case."

She stood there for a very long time, musing. Then, suddenly, her eyes lighted up and she smiled.

"Ah, little mare!" she cried, "now have my wits stood me in good stead! Let us see if this plan will work!"

And forthwith, the Sultan's wife approached the old syce, who was grooming the mare.

"Good fellow," she said, "I wish to ride the mare this morning. Pray have her ready and saddled for me within the hour, and these golden coins shall be yours."

The syce bowed low.

"It will be as you say," he agreed.

So, within the hour, the Sultan's wife set off, riding the white mare. She took the same road that her husband had taken, and reached the next town near dusk.

When she arrived in the town, she saw a fine black stallion standing outside the house of a wealthy merchant. She recognized the horse as that of Sultan Wiil Waal. Her husband, then, was staying the night at the merchant's house.

"Very well," she murmured. "Now we shall see, and God be with us, little mare."

She approached, then, the man who was looking after the black stallion. Dismounting, the Sultan's wife led the white mare up to the syce, and at the same time took a handful of gold coins from her purse.

"Good fellow," said she, "I am journeying to a town near here, to meet my husband, who is a dealer in silks. Now, my husband has long been looking for a stallion fine enough to serve this mare, for, since the mare is of the best Arabian blood, he is determined that her offspring will not be sired by an inferior blood. Do you, therefore, I beg of you, let this black stallion serve the mare, for he is the finest horse I have ever seen. Your master need never know. If you consent, these golden coins are yours."

The syce did not hesitate for long.

"Very well," he said, "it will be as you say, and may God reward you for your generosity, for I have never made so much money so easily."

And so it was as the Sultan's wife had asked.

Then, the Sultan's wife went to an inn, and took a room for the night. When she was in the room, she got out the fine clothes she had brought with her, and donned them. Crimson silks with gold embroidery, robes of exquisite texture and hue, a headscarf of palest blue, shining earrings and necklace of silver, and little red leather slippers.

In this attire, her slim body and soft-featured face looked fairer than could be imagined. She did not tarry in the room, but set out at once for the merchant's house.

When she arrived there, she walked back and forth along the rough stone streets, and as she walked, her body swayed with an unbelievable grace. But she kept her head turned away from the house, and her headscarf was drawn close to her face.

Sultan Wiil Waal was sitting in the house with his friend the merchant, chatting of this and that, the wars with the Ethiopians, and the price of camels. Suddenly Wiil Waal looked up and saw a beautiful woman walking along the street.

"Look there!" he cried to the merchant. "Did anyone ever see a woman with so enchanting a figure, so delightful to walk, so proud a carriage? Who is she, my friend? She must be the most lovely woman in the whole country!"

The merchant peered out into the street.

"You speak truly," he said. "She is indeed charming. But alas, I do not know her name. I have never seen her before."

"Never mind," Wiil Waal said, "whether you know her name or not, I would make love to her tonight. For my senses are aflames with desire for her."

Now it was well known that Wiil Waal had a great fondness for women. Indeed, in each town and each tribal settlement that the good Sultan visited, there was always some girl who took his fancy and whom he forthwith took. His friends and his people knew him well, and the merchant, therefore, agreed to find the woman and ask her, in the name of Wiil Waal, for a meeting that night.

Thus it was, when the night had darkened the town, that Sultan Wiil Waal went to the lovely woman, not knowing she was his wife.

At the moment when she heard his footsteps on the stair, the Sultan's wife blew out the flickering lamp and went to greet him.

"Why is the room in darkness?" Wiil Waal asked her.

"Because I am shy and afraid with so great a Sultan," she replied.

Wiil Waal was satisfied with her reply, and began to caress her body.

But the Sultan's wife drew away.

"No," she said. "Do not touch me."

"Do not touch you?" he cried. "In heaven's name, why not?"

"Because I say so," she replied.

"And why do you say so?" he demanded. "You cannot think I came here to chatter about riddles with you in this fashion."

"No," she said, "but I would first have you give me that ring you wear. Ah, Sultan, not for gain like any common whore, but so I may always remember you, and this night."

Then the heart of Wiil Waal was exceedingly flattered, and he gave her the ring, a silver one with strange letters and charms engraved on it.

And she gave herself to him. And when he had possessed her and taken his full delight of her, and when he had done the ritual ablution, then he fell asleep and lay snoring in the room until morning.

But before dawn had touched the streets with light again, the Sultan's wife arose and went from the inn. Mounting the white mare, she rode speedily away from the town, and made her way home again.

And it came to pass that the woman and the mare both were with young.

Now Sultan Wiil Waal was away from Jigjigga for sixteen months. One day he rode up on his fine black stallion, and there was great rejoicing throughout the city.

When he entered his palace, Wiil Waal discovered that his wife had a sturdy little son of seven months old. And as for the white mare, she had a black colt.

"Now, tell me," Wiil Waal said, and his face was like a thunder-cloud, "how can this be ? I have been away for sixteen months, and my black stallion with me, and yet you and the white mare have both borne young!"

"I have done as my lord commanded," his wife said, with a gentle smile, "and the white mare likewise."

"I did not tell you to be unfaithful to me," said Wiil Waal, "and I did not want the white mare bred by a stallion other than mine!"

And so he raved, without thought or reason. But the wife of Wiil Waal continued to smile, and said nothing. So the Sultan called a council of all the elders of the land.

"Oh ye tribesmen!" he cried, "here is a strange case, to be decided by the wise men and elders of my country. For, look you, I have been away for sixteen months, and my black stallion with me. And yet my wife has borne a son, and my white mare has foaled. What say you, wise men of the Bartire?"

Then the counsellors began to discuss the matter.

"Perhaps the woman and the mare were pregnant before you left," they sugested.

"Ah, no, alas," Wiil Waal replied, "for the day I left was the last day of my wife's monthly sickness, and I had not gone unto her when I departed. Likewise, the white mare was not with young."

Then the elders talked to the wife of Wiil Waal.

"How is it," they said, "that the wife of a Sultan could so disgrace her husband?"

"There is no disgrace," the woman replied calmly. "The boy is Wiil Waal's son. And as for the mare, her colt was sired by Wiil Waal's black stallion."

Then the elders held up there hands in astonishment.

"How can this be?" they shouted. "She is mad, or is lying!"

"It is true," Wiil Waal's wife said. "And God be my witness."

Then, in front of the tribal elders and wise men, she drew forth a silver ring.

"Whose ring is this?" she asked. "And how did I come to possess it?"

Sultan Wiil Waal stared at her in astonishment.

"There was a lovely woman," he said, "the most beautiful woman in all the land. Oh, my wife, it was you?"

Then the wife of the Sultan told her husband what had happened. And the great Sultan laughed loud and long.

"For lo," said he, "she is not only the most beautiful woman in all the land. She is also the most clever. Ah, my beloved, never again will I test your wits. For in my whole kingdom, you are the only person more wise than Wiil Waal!"

9. Wiil Waal and the Wisest Man

Now the Sultan Wiil Waal, who ruled the country between Jigjigga and Harar many years ago, was a man famed for wisdom and for sharpness of wit. Many times did he test his subjects for their cleverness, but never was any man as clever as he. And when Wiil Waal realized that he was the most intelligent man among all the Bartire, pride began to possess him, and he set himself up above men and his vanity grew.

But his wife, who was a woman gifted with wisdom, saw this and was afraid.

It happened that among the Bartire there was a young man named Ali, twenty years of age and blessed by God with a handsome appearance, strength of body and a quick mind.

Now this same Ali became enamoured of the wife of Sultan Wiil Waal and swore he would have her.

So one night he went to her, and with many soft words and much pleading he tried to seduce her.

But the wife of Wiil Waal was not to be seduced. She was pleasant to the boy, and spoke no harsh words to him, but she would not consent to his request.

Ali sat in the room with the wife of the Sultan for several hours, talking to her and saying he could not live without her. But the wife of the Sultan only smiled and shook her head in refusal.

Now it happened that in the room there was a clay vessel that contained some dye liquid. It was the same dye, made from the bark of the 'galol' tree, that the Somali women have always used to colour the bent poles that form the framework of the 'akhals' or grass huts.

As Ali sat there talking, the Sultan's wife took a corner of his white robe, and dipped it in the dye, which was a reddish brown. And Ali did not notice what she had done.

When he was gone, the Sultan's wife went to her husband.

"This night," said she, "I have seen a clever man. Do not be too puffed up with pride, my husband, for another man besides yourself in this tribe has been gifted with persuasive speech and a quick wit. Although he did not succeed in his purpose, which you can guess, his words were nonetheless fair."

Then the Sultan was greatly upset.

"Who is he?" he demanded, "and what is his name, that I may search him out?"

"His name I will not reveal," she said. "But I will tell you one thing. When you meet the tribesmen tomorrow at the council, the man you seek will have one corner of his robe dyed brown."

But it came to pass that Ali, when he unrobed that night, noticed the brown stain, and knew what the Sultan's wife had done. So he went by night and marked the robes of twenty other tribesmen with the same kind of dye.

When the tribesmen of the Bartire gathered the following day, the Sultan Wiil Waal could not keep his mind on the business that was being discussed. He looked constantly for the man with the marked robe.

As he looked, he .found twenty-one men with robes marked brown. And he was greatly distressed. But when he told his wife of the occurrence, she laughed.

"At last," she said, "you have found a man as clever as yourself. Now unbend your pride and lose your vanity, for you are not alone among meñ."

Now the next night, Ali came again unto the Sultan's wife's room.

"Ah, my heart's desire," he said, "have you not relented?"

But the Sultan's wife shook her head, and would not admit him to her bed. Before he left, however, she cut a small piece of cloth from his white robe, and he did not notice what she had done.

When she talked to Wiil Waal that night, she told him of the boy again.

"The boy you seek," she said, "will have a small piece of cloth cut from his robe. And he, mark my words, is a clever man."

But that night, as Ali was taking off his robe, he noticed the small tear, and he knew what the Sultan's wife had done. So he went at once to fifty other members of the Bartire, and spoke with them.

"Our Sultan Wiil Waal," he said, "has commanded that all men of the tribe cut a small piece of material from their robes. This is possibly another of his mad schemes to test our wits, but we must obey him, for certainly he is a good Sultan."

The men believed Ali, and all the fifty cut a small piece of cloth from their robes, just as the Sultan's wife had done with the robe of Ali.

And the next day, when Wiil Waal was consulting his tribesmen, he looked carefully for the man who should have a rip in his garment. And lo, fifty-one men had small pieces of cloth cut from their robes!

When the Sultan told this to his wife, she laughed more than ever.

"Ah, my good Wiil Waal," said she, "let not vanity distort your greatness, for truly now you have seen the action of a clever man."

And it happened that, on the third night, Ali again visited the wife of the Sultan, and begged her to yield to him. Again, she refused. But because she was a clever woman, and talked so entertainingly, the boy almost forgot his desire for her, and they talked together as old friends. That night, the door of the Sultan's apartment was locked, and her husband Wiil Waal did not come to her. And all night long, she sat there with the young man, spinning tales of old battles and ancient feuds, histories and loves, and all manner of stories passed on from generation to generation among the Bartire. And in the morning, he rose up and went back to his own house.

Then the Sultan Wiil Waal came to see his wife.

"Last night," he said, "your door was locked, and I did not behold you all the evening. Tell me truthfully—did you have another man?"

"Sultan," she replied, "many times have you told me you trusted me, and now I will ask you to prove that trust. There was a man in my apartment last night, but upon the Kitab I swear to you that the only thing we did together was to talk. But now I will tell you how you may discover the only clever man in the tribe besides yourself. When you go to the tribal council this day, one man of all the Bartire will be nodding with sleep. This same man was in my room last night, and until morning we talked together, and he did not sleep. He will not be able to conceal himself so cleverly this time, for others in the tribe will not have spent the whole night in chattering."

So it was that Wiil Waal came to the gathering place where all the men of the Bartire were waiting. But when the business of the tribe was being discussed, the Sultan was preoccupied. He kept glancing around, seeking the man who looked as though sleep had not refreshed him the night before. Finally, he saw one young man sitting very quietly among the others, his eyes closed and his head bending wearily. This was the young Ali.

"What is this, my friend?" the Sultan asked the boy, "you look half-asleep."

Then the boy opened his eyes and stared calmly at the Sultan.

"Ah no, Sultan," he replied, "I was not sleeping. I was only thinking."

"And what," asked Wiil Waal, "were you thinking of so earnestly?"

Without hesitation, the boy answered.

"I was wondering," said he, "if the two legs of an ostrich are front legs or hind legs."

Then did the Sultan Wiil Waal laugh heartily.

"You are that man," he said, "who had the boldness to try to seduce a Sultan's wife. And although she refused, and marked you that I might seek you out, three times have you evaded my enquiries. Oh ye Bartire, when I die, this boy will reign as Sultan, for he is as clever as myself."

10. Wiil Waal and the Cowardly Warriors

The Sultan Wiil Waal, who ruled over all the country around Jigjigga, in the old old days, was a great and powerful fighter, and his warriors of the Bartire tribe, of the tribes of Darod, were strong and eager for battle. Many were the times that the warriors of Wiil Waal went out to fight the Ethiopians, and many were the times that they returned back in triumph, bringing huge numbers of Ethiopian shields and Ethiopian camels with them.

But it happened once that the armies of the Sultan met the Ethiopians in battle, and the Bartire were driven back.

Now the tribesmen of Wiil Waal were not accustomed to retreat, and when they saw that they were being overpowered, all their courage suddenly left them, and they would have run away.

So the Sultan Wiil Waal took his youngest son, a fine lad of ten years, and tied him to a tree.

"Will any among the Bartire retreat beyond this tree, and leave my son to the Ethiopians?" he asked. "If one does so, I promise that he shall be beheaded, and I will be the executioner myself."

Then the Bartire did not know what to do. They were afraid to stay and face the Ethiopians, and yet afraid to run away to Jigjigga.

And so they stayed, and fought like leopards, each one swearing to defeat the Ethiopians or die himself. And the Bartire won a great victory that day.

Now the scene of this battle was between Jigjigga and Harar, in the days when the Somalis ruled that land.

11. WIIL WAAL AND THE MIDGAN'S WELL

One day the Sultan Wiil Waal had his brave horse saddled, and rode out among the tribesmen of the Bartire. In his hand he held a white scarf of thin silk.

"Oh ye tribesmen!" he cried, "listen to my words! Outside the city there are many wells, and each is owned by one of you. Now will I bind my eyes with this white scarf, so that I can see nothing. Then will I let my black stallion gallop as fast as he pleases, out beyond the city, among the wells. He is a spirited horse, and wild, and I shall not be able to steer him, since I am blind-fold. But if my horse trips and falls into one of the wells, then the owner of that same well will be beheaded!"

Then all the people set up a mighty groaning and weeping, and everyone was afraid lest his own well be the one into which the Sultan's horse would tumble. And they followed Wiil Waal in a crowd past the gates of the city and out into the country where the wells lay.

When Wiil Waal had reached the place, he tied the white scarf around his eyes. Then he gave the stallion a kick, and they set off at a gallop. Down the slopes of the little hill the stallion raced, running faster than a whirlwind or a dust-devil. And all the people trembled.

But when the Sultan's black horse went close to a well, the owner and all his family began to shout and cry with fear. Screaming, they ran alongside the horse, trying to drive it away.

And each time this happened, Wiil Waal reined up his horse and set off in another direction.

Finally the Sultan's horse drew near the well of a certain Midgan.

Now the Midgan saw quite clearly where the horse was heading. He looked shrewdly at the swift beast and at the Sultan. And he thought his own thoughts.

When the horse was close by the well, all the people pointed and gestured, and told the Midgan to shout and drive the horse away.

"Quiet, ye foolish people," the Midgan muttered, "why should I shout? If the Sultan wishes to break his own neck and that of his horse, let him do so, and may the devil take him!"

Then the people were amazed, and stared at the Sultan's horse with curious eyes, and whispered that the Midgan was mad. But the Sultan reined the horse away from the well, and brought him back to the waiting crowd.

"Lo," said he, "there is only one wise man among you, he who did not shout aloud when my horse approached his well. The Midgan saw that this scarf was thin, and he guessed that I could see through it. The rest of you were ready to believe me a fool, but he knew that I would not risk my own bones and those of my fine steed. The Midgans are a low people, and ye are Somalis, and high-born. But this Midgan, I say to you, has a wisdom from which you could learn much. Observe, ye tribesmen, and profit!"

12. ARAWAILO AND THE CLIMBING OF MIL-MILAC

(NOTE: The Arawailo stories, of which there are many, are among the best-known in Somali folk-literature. One of the stories given here, "The Death of Arawailo", appears in Drake-Brockman's *British Somaliland*[1]. However, Drake-Brockman's version differs in many essentials from this one—the old magician, for example, is not mentioned

1. *British Somaliland*, by R. E. Drake-Brockman, F.R.G.S., (Hurst & Blackett, London, 1912).

at all, and the ritual leading up to Arawailo's death is somewhat different. I have taken Hersi Jama's version of the tale, as it is the one I actually heard myself. Here, as in other cultures, one frequently finds many versions of the same story.)

Many centuries ago, there lived in this country a powerful queen whose name was Arawailo. Now this queen was greatly feared by her subjects, since she was viciously cruel, and wisdom did not enlighten her commands. The chief fury of her hatred was reserved for the men of the tribe, and them she would order to carry out impossible tasks, and would have them put to death if they failed.

One day she called some of the tribesmen before her, and ordered them to go to the mountain which is called Mil-Milac. Now this mountain stands between Marmargedleh and Beyo Anod, and it is the steepest mountain in the whole land. The sides of the cliff at the base of Mil-Milac rise straight up like a wall, and there is no foothold or crevice anywhere, but only rock as smooth as glass.

To this mountain, commanded Arawailo, the tribesmen must go. With them they must take two camels with no mats of any kind on their backs. With these two camels they must climb the steep sides of Mil-Milac, and find some small seeds of the tree that grows on top of the mountain. They must stick the seeds on the camels' bare sides, and return.

The tribesmen were exceedingly afraid. If they succeeded in climbing the dangerous mountain, how could they succeed in making seeds stick to the camels' sides without any mats of any kind, or without a single thing to hold the tiny seeds in place?

When Arawailo dismissed them, the tribesmen went away to consult together.

Now in that tribe there was a very old man, who was a magician. If Arawailo had known of his existence, she would have had him killed, for it was his cleverness that often saved the lives of the tribesmen when the cruel queen ordered them to perform some fantastic deed which seemed to them impossible. The old magician was withered in body from the waist down, and when the people moved their camp, they would bundle him up in mats and conceal him on the back öf a camel, amid all the household goods. The tribesmen now decided that only the old man could save them.

They went to him, therefore, and told him their plight. The old man's sharp eyes gazed at them from his wasted face, and then he sent them away, so that he might think in peace.

After two hours, the magician called all the men back. "And again now," said he, "what did Arawailo order you to do?"

"She has ordered us to take two camels," the tribesmen replied, "with no mats on their backs, and climb the steep sharp hill of Mil-Milac. There we must find some seeds of the tree that grows on top of the mountain, and stick the seeds to the camels' bare sides, and return. How is this possible? Even if we succeed in gaining the top of Mil-Milac, surely the seeds will fall away from the camels' smooth sides on the way down the slope."

Then the magician told them his plan, and they were amazed at his wisdom.

So it was that those same tribesmen followed the old man's advice, and took the camels to a pool close by the mountain, where the water was just drying up, and only mud remained. And the tribesmen made the camels lie down and roll in the mud.

Then the men led the camels up the steep sides of Mil-Milac. They pushed and shoved and slipped, and finally they succeeded in getting to the top of the mountain. There they quickly found the seeds, and stuck them to the still-wet mud on the camels' sides.

When the tribesmen returned, and went to the great queen, and showed her the manner in which they had accomplished their mission, Arawailo was amazed and angry.

"Who told you how to hold the seeds on the camels' sides?" she cried. "You are witless idiots! Someone has helped you in this scheme!"

The men denied it, and claimed that they had thought of the idea themselves. So Arawailo searched through every 'akhal' and in every bush around the camp, but no magician could she find. And so the tribesmen lived, and the old man lived also, and continued to give help and advice to the men of the tribe.

13. THE DEATH OF ARAWAILO

Now the wicked queen Arawailo had a daughter, a gentle copper-skinned girl who had not inherited her mother's cruelty. It happened one time that the old magician decided that Arawailo's mistreatment of the tribe must come to an end. So, although he was at the time a hundred and thirty-five years old, he told the people he would beget a son who would kill the old queen. He went, therefore, to Arawailo's daughter, in great secrecy, and she received him. And she conceived, and bore him a son.

When Arawailo discovered that her daughter was pregnant, she was furious. She did not know who the father was, but she was enraged that her daughter should have had anything to do with any man. And when the child was born, and the queen learned that it was a boy, she was mad with anger.

"Bring me your bastard child," the queen commanded her daughter, "for I am going to have him castrated."

Arawailo's daughter wept and pleaded.

"Please, mother," she cried, "at least spare the boy until he is old enough to. sit up. He is such a tiny child! Spare him I beg of you."

"Very well," Arawailo agreed reluctantly,. "But when he is old enough to sit up, bring him to me."

When the boy could sit up by himself, Arawailo demanded again that he be brought to her.

"Now the time has come," she said, "and the boy will be castrated."

But again Arawailo's daughter begged and cried.

"Spare him, I pray you," she said, "until he is old enough to know something of the world about him, and to speak the name of mother to me."

And again Arawailo agreed.

When the boy was old enough to talk a little, and to say 'mother', and to recognize the camels and the flocks and the grass around him, Arawailo again called for her daughter to bring the child.

"Now the time has come," she said, "and he will be castrated."

"I beg of you," Arawailo's daughter sobbed, "let him be spared until he can walk."

"Very well," Arawailo said. "But then he will definitely be brought to me."

But when the boy could walk, the mother asked that he be spared until he had learned to herd the flocks of sheep and goats, like the other small boys of the tribe. After much persuasion, Arawailo again agreed.

And when the boy could herd the flocks, Arawailo called her daughter.

"The boy is old enough to look after the sheep and goats," she said. "I have done as you asked. Now bring him to me."

"Oh mother," Arawailo's daughter cried, "could you not spare him for a little while longer? Leave him until he is old enough to herd the camels! For he is still such a tiny lad to submit to the horrors of the operation."

"Very well, Arawailo said grudgingly. "So be it. But then there will be no more delay."

When the boy could herd the camels, and had grown tall and handsome, Arawailo's daughter came to the queen to plead for him again.

"I pray you, mother," she said, "spare him for a few more years, so that he may be old enough to carry a spear and shield, and wear a man's robe. Only this one last request do I make, for I shall not ask you again!"

"Very well," Arawailo said. "But do not forget that this is the last time he will be spared."

When the boy had become a man, the old queen again told her daughter that the boy must be castrated, and this time there would be no sparing him.

It was arranged, therefore, that the mother would instruct the boy to take the camels to the wells the next day. Arawailo's followers were to seize him then and carry him away to the royal abode, where the Midgan surgeon would be waiting.

But the boy's mother, although she had been threatened with death if she revealed the queen's plot, told her son what was going to happen. And so that night the boy visited the old magician, his father.

"How can I escape this thing?" the boy asked. "I beg you to help me."

The old man thought for a few moments.

"Make a sheltered place near the wells," he said finally, "and there put fine mats and cushions, and send word to Arawailo to meet you there. I will give you a sharp spear, the finest in all the world."

So the boy went to the wells, and made a shelter of thorn boughs, and placed grass mats and cushions in it. Then he sent word to his grandmother the queen, asking her if she would agree to meet him at the wells, to discuss his future plans.

Arawailo, who was secretly pleased to be able to witness the boy's capture, readily agreed. If he himself had invited her there, she reasoned, he would not become suspicious and run away when he saw her and her followers.

Then the boy returned to the magician. The old man put into his hand a stout spear, bound in brass and made of finest iron, with a shaft of polished 'debii' wood.

"Now," the magician said, "you have a spear. Is it ready?"

The boy held the spear in his hand, to judge the weight of it.

"It is ready," he replied bravely.

"And is it sharp?"

The boy felt along the spear-head with his fingers.

"Yes, it is sharper than a thousand thorns."

"Then," the old man said, "when Arawailo comes into the shelter, throw the spear with one mighty throw, before her followers have time to seize you. When it hits her, take note of what she says. If she cries 'Tol'ai!', come back to me at once, for it will mean that she is a man, after all, and not a woman as she has always pretended. Then you will need help. But if she says 'Allah bie!' or 'Allah hogie!' then she is a woman, and will die without a struggle. Once she is dead, her followers will be afraid, and you need worry no more."

So it was done as the old man advised. The boy went to the wells the next day, and sat inside the shelter. Presently, Arawailo with her followers came to the place. The old queen stepped inside the shelter, and the boy raised the spear to his shoulder and flung it with one mighty throw.

The spear hit Arawailo, and she staggered and fell.

"Allah bie!" she cried.

Thus it was known that, for all her power and cruelty, Arawailo was really a woman. And she died there beside the wells. And the boy became the head of the tribe.

Arawailo was given a great funeral by her people. The women, it is said, mourned her death, and put flowers and green branches on her grave. But the men rejoiced, and to show their hatred of the old queen, they threw stones on her grave. And the name of her place of burial is Elayu.

And until this day, you will still see piles of stones beside a road, shrines to Arawailo, where passing men have thrown a rock onto the heap and passing women have put a green branch there in memory of the queen.

14. THE STORY OF DEG-DER

(NOTE : This is essentially a children's story, although adults enjoy it, too. In the same way that European children are sometimes threatened with "bogey-men", the Somali mother may say to a disobedient child, "Watch out—Deg-Der will get you!" It is said that only a child or a woman will know every detail of the story, although all Somalis know some parts of it. Only two parts of the story are given here, but in its entirety it is supposed to be just the right length to keep a watchman awake throughout the whole night. The tale is said to be very old. "Deg-Der" means "Long Ear".)

A long time ago there lived in this country a woman called Deg-Der. When she married, she was a good woman, and well-schooled in the duties of the household. She cooked the meals and wove grass mats to cover the houses and tended the sheep and goats.

After a time, she bore a child to her husband. It was unfortunate that the child was a girl, but God had willed it so. In due course, Deg-Der bore two more children, and these also were girls, according to God's will. The father of the three little girls was sorrowful at not having sons to support him in the time of his old age, but he kept praying that the next-born would be a boy.

This, however, was not to be. Shortly after the birth of her third child, a strange transformation began to take place in Deg-Der. She showed little interest in her food. and would wander off at nights by herself. Her husband was bewildered, and did not know what to think, until one day, coming home, he was met at the door by Deg-Der, and in her hand she held a long knife.

Her husband, alas, was seen no more. The truth of the matter was that Deg-Der had turned cannibal.

She became more fierce and more horrible to look at as the years went by. The people in that land avoided the 'guri' or settlement of Deg-Der, and when they passed by the place, mothers would clutch at their children, and fathers would hold their spears aloft and ready. In all that land the name of Deg-Der was feared and abhorred, and even the rainclouds stayed away from the sky above her dwelling.

There they lived, year in and year out, the cannibal mother and her three daughters. As the young girls grew older, so did their fear of their mother increase, for they were good creatures with no taste for human flesh. They led a meagre and miserable existence, for no rain ever fell there, and the camels and sheep were thin and wretched-looking. No young men ever came to that place, either, and when the girls had reached a marriageable age, they grew desolate and lonely, and wondered how they might escape.

Now Deg-Der was more ghastly to look at than one could possibly imagine, with her sharp and glowing eyes and her wrinkled skin and her lean body that loped across the country far and wide searching for human quarry. But the most horrible thing about her was one of her ears. This ear was as long as a donkey's, and pointed at the top, and of a terrible keenness. With it she could hear the slightest rustling of a small herd-boy drowsing under a thorn tree, even though he were a night's journey away. When Deg-Der slept, her long ear sunk slowly down, folded over upon itself, and lay still.

In her house, Deg-Der kept three huge clay vessels with tight lids. Two of these vessels were used for keeping water. But the third was used for keeping meat, human meat. This vessel was a marvellously strange one. Only Deg-Der could take the lid off. If anyone else lifted the lid, the jar at once set up a piercing whistle. No matter how far she might have roamed in her hunting, Deg-Der could hear with her long ear the vessel's shrill whistling.

It chanced one day, when Deg-Der was out hunting for her innocent game, a visitor came to the 'guri'.

She was a young girl, this traveller, beautiful and plump and well-formed, and of a coppery gold complexion. But she was dressed in rags.

"I am a poor orphan," she said to Deg-Der's three daughters. "My family is all dead, and now there is no one to look after me. I pray you, in God's name, give me some food and water, for I have been walking these many hours in the hot sun."

The daughters of Deg-Der looked with sympathy on the girl, and gave her some water to drink. They talked with her, and admired her beauty, for she was the first person they had ever seen apart from themselves and their mother.

"Ah, that was good," said the girl as she finished the cup of water. "If I could just have a little more . . . "

And she reached out and took the lid off one of the clay vessels. But in her ignorance, she mistook the vessel, and lifted the top from the one that contained human flesh.

At once a high sharp whistling began. The daughters of Deg-Der stood petrified with terror, not knowing what to do.

"What is the matter?" the girl cried, "and why does the vessel make that strange noise?"

"Alas!" wept the daughters of the cannibal woman, "our mother will hear the vessel's whistling, with her long ear, and will come back at a gallop to kill you and eat you!"

The young stranger began to shriek with fear. At last the three daughters stopped their trembling long enough to hurry the girl into the other room of the house and hide her behind a roll of grass mats.

Soon there was a shout outside the house, and Deg-Der strode in, her eyes horribly alight and her hands grasping her great knife.

"I heard the vessel's warning!" she cried. "Who has come to this house and touched my meat-jar?"

The three girls pretended innocence.

"It is nothing, our mother," they said softly. "We knocked against the jar accidently, when we were cleaning the house, and the lid flew off."

Deg-Der's nostrils dilated, and she sniffed the air, and as she did so a look of great anger came into her hideous face.

"You lie!" she screamed, "I smell the breasts of a fat young girl!"

The three girls shook with fright, but they pretended to be calm.

"It is only our breasts you smell, mother of us," they insisted.

But Deg-Der was still suspicious, and she tramped around the house, searching. Her big ear quivered, trying to detect some sound of a stranger, but so quiet was the young girl that even Deg-Der could hear nothing. Finally her daughters persuaded her to give up looking, and to sit in peace and drink the tea they had prepared for her. Tired with her long run, Deg-Der drank the tea and then fell into a heavy sleep.

Slowly the great knife dropped from her hand. Slowly the great ear sank down and lay still. And when the ear was quite motionless, the three daughters knew their mother was really asleep. Silently they crept towards her. Stealthily they took up the great knife. And speedily they cut the throat of Deg-Der, the terrible cannibal, whose name had been feared for so many years in that land.

Then there followed a great rejoicing. The young girl came out from her hiding-place and thanked with all her soul the three daughters of Deg-Der. And the rainclouds, which had so long kept away from the place, gathered speedily in the sky, and the sweet rain drenched the ground, and the stock drank, and the earth was ripe for growing grass. And the three daughters of Deg-Der danced for sheer joy.

Then there came to that place three young men, all handsome and of good family, and men whose tribes owned many camels. And the three fine young men fell in love with the daughters of old Deg-Der, and asked the three girls to marry them. Two of the girls assented gladly, but the third hung back.

"What is the matter?" asked the young man who loved her. "Do you not care for me?"

The girl sighed.

"Ah, yes," she replied, "I care for you, but my mother became a cannibal after she had her third child, and perhaps the same fate may be in store for me."

But the young man only laughed.

"That is a long time in the future," he cried. "And in any case, it will probably never happen! We are young now, and want each other, and why should we waste our youth?"

So the girl was persuaded, and the three daughters of Deg-Der married the three young men, and there were great celebrations in the land, and much feasting and dancing and singing.

And it came to pass that the third daughter of Deg-Der bore her husband a girl-child. It was God's will, but they prayed that the next-born might be a son. The next child, however, was also a girl. And when the woman became pregnant for the third time, she prayed to God night and day that the child might be a boy. But when she delivered the child, it was a girl.

Then the third daughter of Deg-Der grew worried in her heart.

But her husband only laughed, and told her not to be afraid.

"Such things do not happen to one who is in her right senses," he said. "Surely your mother was mad. Do not be concerned, for you are upsetting yourself without cause."

For a time they were happy together, and began hoping that the next child, if such was given to them, might be a boy. But it was not fated to be.

One day the husband came home and found the door of their dwelling barred against him.

"What is this?" he cried, astounded. "Does my own wife bar the door against me?"

But his wife would not open the door.

"Now then," he said, "if I go and kill a fat sheep for our meal tonight, will you open the door?"

But his wife would still not open the door.

"Suppose I kill a fat camel," the husband pleaded, "the best of my herd, and you may cook the meat for your meal. Will you open the door then?"

But still his wife refused.

Then the husband's face grew wan with fear.

"And if I kill you a fat . . . boy?" he asked.

But the wife would still not unbar the door.

Then the husband's brow grew tight with anxiety.

"And if I kill you a fat . . . girl?" he asked.

But the door remained closed.

Then the husband's heart grew chill with dread.

"If you want none of these things for your meal," he said, "perhaps the one you hunger for is . . myself?"

And then the third daughter of Deg-Der opened the door and met him.

15. THE STORY OF DAROD

(NOTE: The Darod section of the Somali people is one of the two great sections, the other being Ishaak. It is said that all the Somali peoples are descended from these two Arabian nobles. The Ishaak people are those found chiefly in Somaliland Protectorate, the Darod being found in the Protected Area of Ethiopia, in the south of the Protectorate, and in Somalia. I first read this story in Drake-Brockman's book British Somaliland,[1] but the version given here is Hersi Jama's. It is substantially the same as Drake-Brockman's version, although there are a few minor differences—in Drake-Brockman's telling of the story, Dir is accompanied by all his tribesmen to the well, and Darod does not step down from the tree on Dir's shoulders.)

1. British Somaliland, by R. E. Drake-Brockman, F.R.G.S., (Hurst & Blackett, London, 1912).

Darod bin Jibarti bin Ismail was the son of Jibarti bin Ismail, an Arabian nobleman. One day, when Darod was a young lad, his uncle, a Sultan, arranged a great feast, to which the boy was invited. When the guests had assembled, young Darod came to the door, hesitated, and then refused to enter.

The Sultan was very angry. His other guests had been proud to come to his feast, and now his nephew, a mere boy, refused his hospitality. He questioned the boy about it.

"The meat which is prepared for your feast," Darod replied, "has been dressed by a woman who has something of uncleanliness about her, and the sheep from which the meat was taken has something of human flesh about it. I dare not eat, oh Sultan."

The Sultan then summoned all the women of his house, and asked them to explain the boy's words. They would all be put to death at once, he said, if they refrained from telling the truth.

Then all the women were afraid, and looked at one another, but none came forward to explain Darod's words. At last the Sultan's mother came forward and told the truth. She herself was in her monthly sickness, and had prepared the meat for the feast. As for the sheep having something of human flesh about it, at the time when the sheep was a lamb, its mother had died in the drought, and there was no milk for it. The woman who herded the flocks had just borne a child, so she suckled the small lamb from her breast.

When the Sultan heard the woman's words, he was not pacified. He became alarmed at young Darod's powers of vision, and he feared lest his throne be taken away from him by the boy.

And so it came about that the Sultan plotted to kill the young Darod. News of this came to the ears of the boy's father, Jibarti bin Ismail, and he feared for his son's life.

Jibarti then called his four eldest sons to him, and instructed them to take a dhow, and put in it enough food and water for a month, and to take the young Darod in the dhow to the coast of the strange land opposite the Arabian shore.

Thus it came to pass that a dhow was loaded with fresh water, and sheep, enough for a month's food for one man, and in the dhow the four sons of Jibarti bin Ismail set out with their young brother Darod.

When they reached the coast of the shore opposite, the four told Darod that they would all go ashore for a few days, to find out what sort of land it was, according to their father's command. But as soon as they had unloaded the dhow, the brothers left Darod on the shore, and sailed away. And the place where Darod was left is called Bereda.

When Darod saw the dhow sailing away without him, he knew the reason of his father's command. Although he was alone on a strange shore, he did not despair, for the help of God was with him, and the wisdom of Allah was his guide.

The lad set out in search of water, and although it was a barren country, with few trees, he soon found fresh water in plentiful supply, and dug a fine well for himself. Then he set about making a shelter, and with only a stick he dug himself a good cave which would protect him from the wind and sand and sun. The name of that place is "Godka Darod" (Darod's Cave).

Thus Darod lived in his cave for many days and weeks. He drank the sweet water of the well, and ate the flesh of the sheep. But finally it came about that he was reduced to the last sheep. When this was eaten, there remained only the bones. And for the first time, Darod began to despair. But God was with him, and in the morning, when he awoke, the dry bones were covered with meat. The next night, Darod left the bones again in the cave, and in the morning they were clad with flesh. Thus did he live for many days and weeks.

It came to pass one day that Darod saw a girl with her flocks. He went to meet her, and she told him her name was Donbirro, and she was the daughter of Dir, the son of Irrir, and lived in a village nearby. Then Darod asked her if she would like him to water the flocks for her. Donbirro replied that this was impossible, since the nearest well was many days' journey from this place.

But Darod took the sheep and goats and watered them at his well.

Then Donbirro came every day to the place where Darod lived. Every day she gave him some milk from the sheep and goats of her flock, and every day Darod watered the flocks at his well. Donbirro was a beautiful girl, tall and of good bearing, and with soft and comely features, and Darod wanted her for his wife.

But one day the father of Donbirro grew curious, and asked the girl why the flocks would not take water when they returned to the 'guri'. And Donbirro did not reply.

The next day, therefore, Dir, the father of Donbirro, set out with one young man from the tribe to follow the girl when she went out with the flocks.

When they found Donbirro, she was talking with Darod, near the well, and the flocks, having been watered, were resting nearby. When Darod saw the two men, he feared for his life, and so he climbed a huge tree that stood close by the well, having first covered the mouth of the well with a large flat stone. And that tree is known as "Lanta Ful" (The Branch He Climbed), and it is standing yet.

The father of Donbirro approached with the other man of the tribe, and when they saw the girl and Darod, they were very angry. Then they saw the well, and the flocks resting, and they coveted the well for the use of the tribe, and wished to take it away from Darod.

And so the two men strove to take away the stone from the well. But Darod was beloved of God, and the stone would not move. The two men struggled with it, and shoved with all their strength, but to no avail. Then they called for Darod to come down from the tree, but Darod, knowing they meant him no good, refused.

Finally Dir, the father of Donbirro, asked Darod what price he would take to come down from the tree and remove the heavy stone from the well, so that the tribe might use the water. Darod replied that he would come down and remove the stone and give the well to the tribe for their own use, if Dir, the father of Donbirro, would let him marry the girl. For she was beautiful, and graceful, and of good temper, and Darod wanted her for his wife.

Then the father of Donbirro told Darod he might have the girl, and so Darod consented to descend from the tree.

But Darod told the two men that if he jumped from the tree he would break his bones. Therefore he asked the men to come and stand beneath the tree that he might step down on their shoulders.

The one man refused, and was proud and haughty, but Dir, who was the head of his tribe, came and stood beneath the tall tree, and Darod stepped on his shoulders and came down to the ground. And it was a sign of peace between them.

And Darod approached the well, where lay the flat stone which the two men could not move, and he kicked away the stone lightly with one foot. And the tribesmen were amazed.

Then Darod married Donbirro, and from her he had five sons. And Darod lived out his life in that land, and from him are descended many great men and many tribes. And the tribes of Darod are the Warsangeli, the Dolbahanta, the Mijertein, the Ogaden, the Abasgul and the Bartire.

And Darod was beloved of God, and had great wisdom, and lived the life of a Muslim. And Darod went among the people and spoke to them the words of the Prophet (Upon whose Name be Praise), and turned away from their idols, and towards Allah, the Merciful, the Compassionate.

16. THE STORY OF SHEIKH AU BARKHADLEH

(NOTE: This is Hersi Jama's version of the story,

which he obtained from a number of the local elders. **The** name "Mohamed Hanif", however, I have taken from *A Grammar of the Somali Language*, by J. W. C. Kirk, B.A. (Cambridge University Press 1905), where an account of the Yibirs' ancestor is published in the Yibir dialect, together with an English translation. The Yibir version of this part of the story differs a good deal from the Somali version which is given here.)

In the time of the Prophet Mohamed (On Whose Name Be Peace), there lived in Mecca a man named Ali Ibn Abi Dalib. He was a noble man and a great warrior, and he fought bravely in the wars that were then taking place in Mecca against the Christians. Now this same Ali Ibn Abi Dalib married Fadima 'Rasuul (Saint Fadima), who was the daughter of the Prophet Himself.

Fadima 'Rasuul bore two sons to Ali, and the names of the two were Hussein and Hassan.

And Yusuf Khounein, he who became later known as Sheikh au Barkhadleh, was the son of Hussein, the son of Ali Ibn Abi Dalib, and he was descended on his mother's side from the Prophet Mohamed.

Now, when Sheikh Yusuf Khounein was a grown man, he decided to leave Mecca and travel to far lands to spread the words of the Prophet among pagan peoples.

And so it was that he came to the place where Mogadiscio now stands. And he went ashore and walked among the people.

"Who are you?" they said unto him, "and what is your business in this land?"

"I am a Sheikh," Yusuf Khounein replied, "and I have come to bring you the words of the Prophet Mohamed and the Peace of Faith."

And he lived among them, and taught them, and they turned away from their idols and towards Allah, the Merciful, the Compassionate.

Then Sheikh Yusuf Khounein left that place and travelled to the Rahan Wein people, south-west of Beledweina.

And he went among the people.

"Who are you?" they said unto him, "and what is your business in this land?"

"I am a teacher," Sheikh Yusuf replied, "and I have come to turn you from the path of idolatry and sin."

And he lived among them and taught them the Faith, and they became Muslims. Now Sheikh Yusuf stayed in that place a hundred years, and his teachings included even the complex books of Theology and the Laws.

Then it came to pass that Sheikh Yusuf Khounein travelled to the country west of Addis Ababa.

"Who are you?" the pagan people asked, "and why do you come here?"

"I am a teacher," he answered, "and I have come to publish the Muslim religion among you, for behold, there is no god but God!"

And he taught them for many years, and the Ethiopians called him Jima Bajifa.

Then Sheikh Yusuf Khounein went to Harar, and walked among the people, and taught them. For three hundred years he lived there, and demanded nothing from any man, but only the freedom to speak the words of the Prophet unto them. And the people in that place stopped their idol-worship, and broke their idols, and became Believers.

Now it came to pass that Sheikh Yusuf Khounein heard of the Esa people, who were then pagans and knew not of the One God.

"Many people there are in that country," he said, "and they are wild men, who live in idolatry and uncleanliness. And lo, they have no prophet. I must go among them."

So he travelled to Bulhar. There was no town nor any market-place there in those days. He lived there for a few years, and then travelled to a place between Bulhar and Berbera. And all the while he taught the people, and showed them the way of the Faith.

Then it came to pass that Sheikh Yusuf Khounein travelled to a place close to where Hargeisa now stands.

And the land was sorrowful, for it was a desert land and there had been no rain there for many months. The wells were dry, the grass was shrivelled, the camels and flocks were thin and the people lived in suffering and bitterness.

But on the very day that Sheikh Yusuf Khounein arrived, the rain-clouds gathered and the rain fell, and the 'tugs' flowed like rivers night and day.

"It is a sign," Sheikh Yusuf said unto the people.

And he gave thanks unto God, Lord of the Worlds. And all the people marvelled.

And because it rained on the day that Sheikh Yusuf Khounein came to that country, the people called him "Au Barkhadleh", which means "The Lucky One". And thenceforth he was known as Sheikh au Barkhadleh.

He lived among the people there, teaching them the Muslim faith and opening their eyes to the wisdom of the Prophet. And they broke their idols and turned towards Allah, the Lord of men, the King of men, the God of men.

And Sheikh au Barkhadleh married a woman of that country, and she bore him one child. It was a girl child, who died when she was four months old. And Sheikh Au Barkhadleh's wife bore him no more children.

The years passed, and Sheikh Au Barkhadleh was an old man and well-respected. Many hundreds of years had he spent in travelling and teaching.

"Henceforth I will travel no more," he said unto the people, "but will stay here, and build a big mosque, and here will I die, when God wills it."

So he had a mosque built there, and the name of the place was Dogor, on the banks of the Tug Marodijehh.

Because Sheikh Yusuf was loved of God, he could see visions, and could tell what was happening the same day in Mecca and Medina. In dreams, God showed him wisdom, and angels appeared to him while he prayed. The people respected and loved him, and the word of his teachings spread throughout all that land.

Now it happened one time that a certain Mohamed

Hanif came to the place where Sheikh Au Barkhadleh lived. Mohamed Hanif was a Yibir, one of the outcast peoples, those who are learned in magic and sorcery. Mohamed Hanif posed as a great Sheikh. He questioned the authority of Sheikh Au Barkhadleh, and sought to drive him away from that country.

"Go from this land," Sheikh Au Barkhadleh commanded the Yibir, "and go from my people, for you are an impostor, and you will not prevail against me."

But Mohamed Hanif would not go.

"I am the greater man," he said. "Be thou afraid."

"I am never afraid," Sheikh Au Barkhadleh replied, "for God is my protection. But if you are as great as you say, let me see what marvellous things you can accomplish."

Now there was a small hill near the mosque at that place.

"I will go through the hill," Mohamed Hanif said, "and then you will see the power of my magic."

So Mohamed Hanif the Yibir walked through the hill, and when he emerged on the other side all the people were amazed and afraid. But Sheikh Au Barkhadleh challenged the Yibir to go through the hill again. Mohamed Hanif did so, and again Au Barkhadleh challenged him to perform the act of magic once more.

The Yibir walked into the hill for the third time. But this time Sheikh Au Barkhadleh prayed aloud to God to let the earth hold the Yibir so that he might never emerge.

And God answered the prayers of Sheikh Au Barkhadleh, and the earth caught hold of the Yibir, and the hill swallowed him, and he was never seen again.

Then all the people marvelled at the good Sheikh.

But the Yibir people were angry. They came to Au Barkhadleh and demanded compensation for the death of Mohamed Hanif. So the Sheikh agreed that a compensation should be paid.

"The Yibir people," he said, "will have the right to collect a toll from the Somali people. Whenever a son is born to a Somali family, or whenever a marriage takes place, my people will pay thy people a certain sum. Thus it will be from this time forward, until the end of the world."

And so it is that the Somali people pay a sum of money to the Yibirs whenever a son is born or a marriage takes place, and the Yibirs give in return an amulet with protective powers, containing verses from the Qoran, as a sign of the agreement that Sheikh Au Barkhadleh made with the Yibir people many hundreds of years ago. And if a Somali does not adhere to the bargain, the Yibirs will seek to steal the male child or will cause the men concerned to go mad.

Now Sheikh Au Barkhadleh lived in that place many years, and the people listened to his teachings, and he brought the Muslim faith to them.

Finally, by God's will, he died, an old and respected man, and the people buried him. And every year pilgrims visit the place where the good Sheikh Au Barkhadleh is buried.

17. THE STORY OF SHEIKH ISHAAK

(NOTE : There are many different versions of the story of Sheikh Ishaak. The paraphrase given here uses details both from the version told to me by Hersi Jama and that found in a translation of some old writings from Arabia which were made available to me. A description of the tribes of Ishaak appears in British Somaliland by R. E. Drake-Brockman, F.R.G.S. (Hurst and Blackett, London, 1912). I have followed Drake-Brockman in the proper names of two of Ishaak's sons, Ahmed and Abdullah. In the old Arabic version of the tale, the real name of "Arap" is given as "Ali", rather than Ahmed, and the real name of "Toljalla" as "Mohamed", rather than Abdullah.)

Sheikh Ishaak bin Ahmed, the founder of the Ishaak tribes, came to this country from Arabia. He had lived in Mecca, and he set out to carry the Muslim faith to far countries. He travelled on foot through Egypt, the Sudan and the country that is now Eritrea. Finally he came to Zeilah. He was fifty-seven years old when he arrived in this country, and he stayed at Zeilah for eleven years, teaching the people the words of the Prophet (On Whose Name Be Peace). And they turned away from their idols, and became Muslims.

Then Sheikh Ishaak travelled to Harar, and there he stayed many years, preaching the Qoran and instructing the people.

Now in those days Sheikh Au Barkhadleh was still alive, and was teaching the Muslim faith throughout this land. When Sheikh Ishaak learned that the old man was still living, he refused to go and see him, and instructed his followers not to tell the old Sheikh of his presence in the country.

"For it is fated," he said, "that one of us shall start a new race of people, who will inherit the land, while the other will die and leave no sons. Sheikh Yusuf Khounein is an older man than I, and a great and famous teacher. If he knew it had been revealed to me that one of us would father a new race, would he not beg God to allow him to be the one?"

And so it was that the two Sheikhs never met, although both spread the Prophet's words throughout the land.

Then it came to pass that Sheikh Ishaak bin Ahmed left Harar and went on the Haj. When he had made the Pilgrimage, he returned to Harar and taught there again for three years. And his total number of years in Harar, before and after his Pilgrimage, numbered twenty-five.

One day it came to pass that God revealed to Sheikh Ishaak what his future should be. And Ishaak was told to travel along the seashore until he came to a place where his spear, being thrust into the ground, could not be pulled forth again.

So it was that Sheikh Ishaak set out along the seashore, and at each village he set his spear into the sand,

and each time he pulled it forth again. Then he came to Mait, and he thrust his spear into the ground. When he tried to pull it forth, he could not. So he knew it was the appointed place for him to live and teach. And he was ninety-five years old at that time.

Now in those days the people at Mait were a wild people who worshipped idols and lived without any knowledge of the world, and clad themselves only in the skins of animals.

But Sheikh Ishaak taught them that there is no god but God. He spoke the words of the Prophet unto them, and taught them the Laws. And they became Muslims, and broke their idols, and followed the words of the Prophet, and ate clean food.

Sheikh Ishaak built a mosque in that place, and began a Qoranic School. He taught the people how to trade, and in a few years the village grew and the dhows from Arabia began to call there. Mait became a large port, and the trade was in aromatic gums.

Now Sheikh Ishaak bin Ahmed took a wife. Her name was Magado, and she was the daughter of Magad. Many years passed, and she bore no children.

So Ishaak married an Ethiopian slave-girl. Her name was Hannifa, and she bore four sons. The name of the eldest son was Abdullah, and his nick-name was Toljalla.

Then Magado, the wife of Ishaak, bore him twin sons, and their names were Ahmed, nick-named Arap, and Ismail, nick-named Gerhajis.

Magado died, and Sheikh Ishaak married another daughter of Magad. And she bore him two sons, Abdurrahaman, whose nick-name was Awal, and Ayoub.

The three younger sons of Hannifa joined their families with those of their elder brother Toljalla to form the Habr Toljalla tribe

And the sons of Magado formed the Arap tribe and the Habr Gerhajis (which is the Habr Yunis and the Eidagalla tribes together). And the two sons of Sheikh Ishaak's third wife joined their families together to form the Habr Awal tribe. And the tribes of Habr Awal, Habr Yunis, Eidagalla and Arap are together called Habr Magadleh, because they are descended from the .two daughters of Magad.

Sheikh Ishaak lived many years at Mait, and when he died he was a hundred and eighty-five years old. He was a great teacher, and brought the wisdom and the light of the Prophet's words to this country. And he founded a new race of people, as it had been revealed to him, and his sons inherited the land.

PRINTED IN EAST AFRICA BY W. BOYD & CO. (PRINTERS) LTD., NAIROBI.